TORNADO!

UP FROM THE DEBRIS

to *Thank* *God*

Complier: Fern, Mrs. Eric Unruh

Editor: Barb, Mrs. Roy Boese

Front Cover Photo: Courtesy of Andy Fischer

Back Cover Photo: Courtesy of Mark Humpage

Cover Design: Amos Yost and Jim L. Friesen

Book Design and Layout: Jim L. Friesen

Printed in the United States of America by Mennonite Press, Inc., Newton, Kansas.

International Standard Book Number: 978-0-9801971-9-8

Library of Congress Control Number: 2008900162

Dedication

To every home who,
when facing the storm,
will look to God for help.

Contents

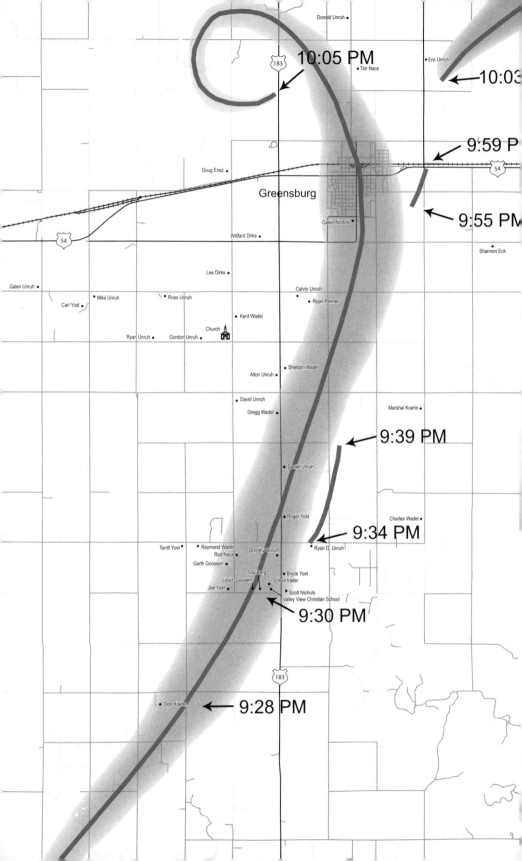

Prologue

May 4, 2007 didn't seem unusual in any way at the farm of Roger and Marsha Yost. They were involved in usual spring activities. But as they sat at supper that night with their married son Terrill and his young bride Krista, rain began pelting the windowpanes, quickly turning to hail stones that pounded the house with ferocious intensity.

"There's a lot of power behind that hail," someone said. "Let's go out to the screened porch to watch for a while."

A sheet of white hail obliterated almost everything. Lightning flashed incessantly, and the thunder rolled. The barrage of hail produced a deafening cacophony of sound.

"Look, somebody's parking under the elm tree at the end of the driveway," someone commented above the noise of the hail. The hail was so thick they couldn't see who it was.

"It'd be a bad night to be out in a storm like this," commented another.

Suddenly a tremendous blast of wind hit their house. The electricity went out, and they were in blackness. The storm was intensifying. The wind tore at the house, hail slammed against the siding. Would the windows break?

Terrill took hold of Krista's shoulders and propelled her to the stairs. Unheeding of her protests that they were going too fast in the dark, he continued to shove her down the stairs. "We've got to get down there!" he urged. They stepped into the storage room.

While the rest headed down, Roger stood at the back door and motioned with his flashlight for whoever was out there to come in.

He held the door open. How would those people get in? Hail was pounding down...Suddenly there was a lull in the hail. Ryan and Rachelle Unruh jerked their car doors open, and grabbing Dylan and Reese, their two little boys, made a wild dash for the open door. Safely in the house, Roger shone the flashlight so they could rush downstairs.

"Quickly! Downstairs!" Roger encouraged. Hurrying down the steps into the basement, they joined the rest of the family who were busy pulling things out from under the steps so they could take shelter there.

Before they got a space cleared under the steps, their ears began popping. The noise of the storm was deafening. Debris blew in the basement windows.

"Get in there! Get in there! Now! Now!" everyone cried. How did they know? What did they hear? They didn't stop to analyze the noises they heard. They just knew they had to, for the sake of their lives.

They jammed in - all ten of them - practically sitting in each others' laps, and the crashing grew louder.

All nature now began to vent its fury. The power of the tornado and the helplessness they felt were impossible to describe. Repeated crashing joined the banging of hurled objects above them. Ryan and Roger were audibly praying. "Our Father in Heaven, we pray for Your protection. Please keep us safe through this storm..."

The walls fell in on the stairs they had just used.

"Oh God! Oh God!" "Our house just went!" "We don't have a house!" "Just pray!"

Krista felt her feet bouncing off the floor like a basketball as she shook with fright. Yet, in spite of the chaos and fear, they later marveled at their inward calm.

"How terrible if one of us gets sucked out of here!" thought Krista.

Suddenly all became eerily still.

"The eye of the storm..." someone was saying. But the calm was quickly shattered by even more ferocious pounding of the wind. Once again they felt the thuds and crashing of flying debris as if recklessly thrown about. Walls were ripped apart, and the eerie screech of nails yanked out by brute force of the wind added to the deafening roar above them. Wood splintering, ripping, banging, colliding — would it never end?

Finally, finally, after what seemed like an eternity, the wind slowed and the crashing ceased.

"It's over!" Roger breathed with relief. "We're alive!"

"What if this is just the eye of the storm?" one of the ladies asked anxiously.

Despite their fears, one by one they pulled themselves out of their cramped cubbyhole and tried to step over the debris scattered around them. Helping each other maneuver their way out, they looked up. Nothing but open air!

"Mommy," a little voice said, "I wish Jesus was down here with us."

"He is, Dylan, He is. He was right here keeping us safe..."

Chapter 1

A Spring Evening Picnic Disrupted

We are just a common farm community where in winter, boys still play hockey on the farm pond. In the summer, picnics are the reward of a hot day's work out in the hay field. Friday, May 4, 2007, was just one of those ordinary days. On this evening, a large group of farm families had gathered for a potluck supper at Anthony and Carol's place and the good-natured fun began.

"Hey, Anthony, are we going to get rained out again?" Anthony was being reminded of how often their picnics got rained out. Rain was unusual in this part of the country, as drought had dogged the community the last few years. The hard-working farmers didn't mind being rained out one little bit.

We gathered under a shade tree, where tables were set up, laden with delicious home-cooked food brought by the ladies. The food table was amply loaded, and the men relaxed under the tree with good-natured talk.

"Remember the sound of the rain on the tin roof the last time we had a picnic here?" someone asked. "Maybe a little rain would help to replenish the water table."

The drought was on everybody's minds. Even youth girls took the time to check on North Rattlesnake Creek the last time it rained. Yes, the whole community looked to the clouds for refreshment.

The taco salad was especially tasty that night. Tina talked about the forecast for severe weather, but nobody seemed worried about it. We often hear about weather watches in the spring and don't necessarily keep close track, because, so often, nothing comes of them.

Toward the end of the meal, tiny rain drops began sprinkling over the picnickers. Left-over food was quickly stowed in the vehicles, and the mothers moved inside to visit, while the children and youth played volleyball in the shed.

The hot, humid weather produced a rather lazy volleyball game. Fathers stood around, watching the game and 'chewing the breeze,' or a stalk of grass. Friends, good food, and shouts of happy children in the balmy night air made for a lovely evening.

In the kitchen, Carol stashed the last of the silverware away while the ladies chatted. When the last of the meal was put away, everyone settled down in the family room, watching the little children play. Life is so full of lessons for the little ones when the toys need to be shared. Marshal and Carey were preparing to leave for a mission term in New Mexico, and Carey was telling us about her latest packing challenges.

That morning, Dick McGowan, a storm chaser from Olathe, KS, called up an old buddy from high school he hadn't chased with since the previous year.

"This weekend will be the mother of all outbreaks," he warned him.

Dick took off work at noon on Friday and met Derek Shaffer, and then they picked up Darin Brunin in Ottawa. They headed to St. John, Kansas, and chatted with some chasers from England for awhile.

There were two options...go north or south. After much debate, they decided on the dry line near the KS/OK border. Thinking they could catch the Woodward, OK storm, they drove into Coldwater and continued south. They didn't have much time. Three storms were fighting for dominance. There was a beautiful LP (northern storm) which was stacking some plates — until it raced away. The southern storm eventually got the dominance and the warning of "tornado" was issued.

Speeding west out of Coldwater, they noticed the biggest inflow band Dick had ever seen, feed into a monster wall cloud near Sitka. It was truly a sight to see — a nice back-lit updraft with a rotating wall-cloud and a tail-cloud feeding into that... a chaser's dream. They immediately reported an imminent tornado via spotter network. Eight to ten minutes later, they witnessed the first brief cone touch down. Again, they reported this via spotter network.

Three separate areas of rotation were all eager to put down a tornado. After the cone lifted back up, the mesocyclone to the northwest of it formed a nicely condensed funnel and would subsequently put down a large stovepipe. By this time, it was getting dark outside, and they were losing the storm, even though it was only traveling at twenty to thirty mph (a chaser's dream!)

A new area of interest was emerging; a southern supercell in the process of creating one of the most violent cyclic supercells that even the most veteran of chasers could recall in quite some time. At that moment, Dick was content with the "day before the day" setup and had already considered it a success from his personal point of view. Little did any of them know that history was in the process of being written, and the lives of the residents in a small Kansas farming community and others surrounding it would be forever changed.

A storm chaser can and will make up any excuse to head out any given day, and they decided they would just be setting up for the following day because models were hinting at an even bigger event, in generally the same area. For Dick, personally, it was mental torture watching earlier tornado events in the year unfold with his absence, while he was grounded due to mandatory responsibilities.

Everything went so quickly, yet slowly at the same time; from enjoyable chasing immediately into white-knuckle, muddy-road driving, which instilled fear into each of them in just a matter of moments. They purposely wedged themselves in-between two, strong, low-level mesocyclones, one of which spawned a very mature, stout, stovepipe tornado to their northwest and was appearing to be giving birth to its first funnel cloud about three hundred yards in front of them. Even as they entered dusk, they could watch detailed motion of the funnel cloud, and shortly after, a tornado, which would continue on and be directly responsible for the first official EF-5 tornado that would nearly wipe the town of Greensburg off the map!

The tornado first touched down about three hundred yards in front of them, skipping along the ground for several minutes before establishing itself as a stout stovepipe. Suddenly, their northbound paved road turned into mud. The storm chasers kept thinking that their chase would soon be over, but Dick somehow managed to keep it steady or fishtail enough to overcorrect the car back into the road. The tornado was by now strengthening, as it was showing signs of stronger multiple vortices now dancing around what seemed to be a developing wedge tornado. (Wedge is defined as a tornado that is wider than it is tall.) While gaining ground on them, they were losing it, which was probably a good thing because it was widening itself now at the base.

Chapter 2

"Pray, Mama!" ① RAIN ② HAIL ③ DARKNESS

9:10 pm. The calm of the evening was shattered with the ringing of the phone. It was Carol's sister.

"There's been a tornado spotted one mile south of your place!" she reported.

With this news, almost the entire group of happy picnickers ran downstairs to the basement for shelter. Rain was slashing across the yard, and then hail began to pummel the ground. Suddenly, the electricity went off, and all was in darkness — no more weather monitor.

"If you step outside the front door, you can see a tornado on the ground!" somebody called.

Fourteen-year-old Titus had an appreciation for storms, just like his dad. When he heard there was a tornado on the ground, it didn't take him long to go up the steps. What they saw was a magnificent sight! In between lightning flashes, they could see a dark wall making its way across the horizon. Little funnels danced up and down alongside it. They hesitated to call the wall a tornado. Never before had they seen one of such gigantic proportions! The little ones beside it were the right shapes, but this wall was too wide to resemble a tornado. There was suddenly an urgency to pray for those in the path of the storm.

Some of the fathers watched the weather radar on their cell phones. Dan hadn't been at the picnic, and he was calling his wife, Deb; Jessica had gone to Pratt with the Howard Eck family to escape the tornado, and she was communicating with Charles and Sherri. Severe weather was visible around Don and Shana's place. Anthony gave them a call to see if they were in a storm.

HAIL

whistling /screaming

Don and Shana had been in Wichita for the day. They stopped to pick up their children and groceries and got home around 7:00 p.m. to eat a late supper while the children went out to do the calf chores. It was sprinkling lightly.

"Good. Maybe it will rain," Shana thought to herself.

The electricity went off for about 10 minutes and then came back on. There was lightning and thundering enough for Don to call his brother at Texline, so he could hear some 'good Kansas thunder.' When it started to hail, Don ran out to park Alton's pick-up in the shed and put the dog, Sassy, in the garage. On his way back inside, he looked up and saw the lights in the house were on again. It had suddenly turned into a calm and beautiful evening.

As he walked toward the house, he spotted a baseball-sized hailstone among the golf-ball sized and picked it up for the children to see. Anthony called and told them there was a tornado headed their way. Would it amount to anything? Residents of Kansas are accustomed to many warnings.

Don had always enjoyed storms. He could remember a mighty thunderstorm going directly overhead once when they were living in a rented house. He had thoroughly enjoyed the thunder nearly shaking that old house. Their new house seemed a little sturdier. With another storm coming and the electricity on again, Don and his oldest son Tanner went to take showers.

Now the hail began pounding the house. Above the noise of the storm, Shana and the children scrambled downstairs to shelter. The wind was whistling around the yard. Shana glanced up in time to see the park bench scooting across the deck. She ran up the stairs to tell Don to come downstairs with them; then she warned Tanner to get out of the shower, too.

Nine-year-old Taryn looked up the stairs and screamed when the deck door flew open. Shana quickly took the children to the furnace room and then ran back up to yell at Don again. She was thinking 'wind' the first time she ran up to warn Don, but now she was thinking 'tornado!'

The wind was a constant, loud, high-pitched screaming and whistling sound. She huddled there in the furnace room, praying with the children for Daddy to make it safely down. Twice, three-year-old Logan clutched his arms around his mother. "Pray, Mama!" he cried.

Pressure

⊷◆⊷

"There's a storm coming!" Shana called to Don through the bathroom door.

"She's probably a bit shook up," he mused to himself.

But when she came back the second time with more urgency in her voice, he knew the storm must be worsening. He turned off the fan, and heard the howling of the wind. Did the children leave a door open, he wondered?

As he opened the bathroom door, he felt tremendous pressure outside. The bathroom door ripped off and slammed across his eye. Noticing the deck door was open, Don ran back for clothes, leaping onto the bed to get to them, because the chest of drawers was lying across his path. It was dark as he hurried through the broken glass, missing more steps than he hit. The boisterous force of the wind literally blew him down the stairs.

Frantically searching the downstairs bedrooms for his family, he finally found them in the furnace room.

"Taryn, are you here?" he called anxiously, straining to see in the darkness.

"Yes, Daddy, I'm here," a scared little voice came back clearly.

"Trey — are you here?" "Jaci?" "Logan?" "Tanner?"

What a relief to hear each one of their five children answer when he called them by name!

As the family huddled together around the furnace, they began to pray. The storm was wreaking havoc with their new house, but their thoughts were, 'a house is only a house.'

"God, You can take our new house — just please, spare our lives!"

The storm raged on. They watched the door to the furnace room being sucked in and out, in and out. Would it survive the pressure?

⊷◆⊷

The mud road now curved back to the east for the storm chasers, which put the newly-organized wedge tornado to their north-northeast about two or three miles away. They kept heading east, Dick trying not to watch the tornado too much because the slightest distraction could land them in the ditch. He could only coax twenty to thirty miles per hour out of his vehicle on the muddy road.

Two miles further down the road, Dick began to feel ill. His ears began to ring. Instinct told him, "Something's wrong!" A police officer's patrol car flew past them and then turned back around.

Dick McGowan and his friends were now alone on a muddy road a few hundred yards away from a very large tornado. They watched as it hit a farm, power flashes illuminating the violent rotation. They could see the farm was severely damaged. A major gas leak sprang from a gas tank in the adjacent field. Slowly picking their way along, they narrowly drove underneath downed power lines. The sheriff drove headlong into the power lines as he tried to find a way to the farmhouse.

The road they were now on was very muddy. Randy Hicks flew by them in his vehicle, fishtailing his way to the wedge. Fifteen miles of white-knuckle driving on the lonely, muddy road brought them back to HWY 183, and closer to the wedge of the tornado.

———————

9:28p.m. Meanwhile, down in the furnace room with his family, Don could tell the storm was abating. He heard the phone ringing. It was Anthony.

"Are you alright? Did you get hit?" was his question.

"Yes, we've been hit, but we're all okay," Don assured him.

"Really? You were hit?" Anthony wanted to make sure Don wasn't joking as he often did.

"We'll be right over," he told him.

Don and Shana and their family cautiously emerged from the furnace room. Surveying the damage, they saw new walls had holes where doors had slammed right through them. A piece of living room furniture had tumbled and broken another hole. New cabinets were pitted and scratched. Except for the office window, every window on the main floor was broken. Don opened the garage entry door and was amazed to find no garage. The vehicles that had been there were demolished.

How extensive was the damage? As yet, Don didn't know. But, being a member of the Christian Disaster Relief committee, a tremendous load would settle on him with cleanup work throughout their community. Neither did he realize that the tornado was headed toward the school. Don was also the chairman of the school board.

Many of the survivors that night would later often look to Isaiah 40:29 for the needed strength. "He giveth power to the faint; and to them that have no might he increaseth strength."

Chapter 3

Unbelievable Devastation. "Do We Have A Home?"

Back at Anthony's, the group of picnickers crowded into Anthony's back hallway around the landline telephone. Cell phone service was sporadic.

The news that Don's place had been hit was sobering. The adults mouthed the news to each other. Wide-eyed children didn't miss a thing. After piecing together bits and pieces of information, they sidled up to their parents, looking for confirmation or re-assurance. Parents weren't able to assure the little ones that night that everything would be okay. None of us knew if we had a home anymore. None of us knew until the next day who had survived the night.

We used to be able to tease our children with their little fears of storms, "What makes you think you are so special that a tornado would choose to hit you? Do you know of anyone a tornado has hit? Chances are not very likely."

But on the night of May 4, we were hit with the reality of an actual life nightmare. Don and Shana had barely moved into their new house. Now it was no longer a nice, new home. The news came that Don had been hurt. What a relief when we were reassured that he would be okay.

"I'm going with Anthony to board up windows at Don's house!" Eric tersely told Fern when he burst in the back door. Jason, Tristan, and Andy jumped into the vehicle with them. As the five of them followed the path the tornado had left, they could still spot the tornado west of HWY 183, heading north.

Was it safe for the men to leave under these conditions? There was some anxiety, but it was the right thing for them to do. Anthony, being a man of action, wouldn't hesitate to help out a brother-in-law.

A large tree lay across the road that the men couldn't get around. They tried the next mile road. Tall highline power poles had fallen there. They saw sparks around the wires. A Coldwater fireman, out storm spotting, told them to go ahead and drive across the downed wires.

"Just don't get out of your pickup when you drive on them!" he warned them.

Rather than take the risk, the men sped through the grassland, arriving safely at Don's farm.

———— ◆ ————

As the storm chasers reached HWY 183, they were stressed to see others had stopped their vehicles in the middle of the highway.

"PULL. OVER. TO. THE. SIDE," they thought in exasperation while they dodged the vehicles in their way.

About eight miles south of Greensburg they witnessed the first of the damage. The initial damage path was totally unbelievable. Trees were stripped bare. Nearly every gas line was leaking across the highway, and most structures were severely damaged. Cows, injured badly, walked around in shock on the highway. Vehicles were tossed around like Lego blocks. Everything seemed surreal.

HWY 183 was littered with all manner of debris. Power lines lay across the road. A man appeared, waving his arms in search of help. They stopped their vehicle beside him.

"Can we help you?" they asked the worried man.

"Yes! I just crawled out of my basement. We were badly hit. Could you go back south to see if my relation got hit? The name is Unruh."

Dick measured his words. He didn't have the heart to tell this man that his relative's house was destroyed by the tornado. Furthermore, driving back south would have taken them back through the power lines and leaking gas lines. To do so would risk their lives. He pulled into Mr. Unruh's driveway, turning on his flashers until another car approached.

It was storm chaser Dan Robinson, with Fabian Guerra behind him. After telling them the situation, they decided to drive north in tandem, zigzagging their way through power lines on the road. At one point a pole covered the whole road, except for a small area on the west side of the ditch. They gunned their vehicles through the ditch and barely made it through.

Continuing to the next road block, they saw that poles and lines covered the road diagonally, this time with the lines blocking the east side of the road, and the power pole blocking the west. Two vehicles had stopped ahead of them; they were the third. By skillful maneuvering, they managed to pull up the power lines so the cars could drive through.

After Mr. Unruh directed them to his relation's house, they heard from Matt Jacobs that Greensburg had taken a direct hit, and they went to see if anyone needed help. Dick saw Sean Wilson on a dirt road and told him about Greensburg. Cautiously, both vehicles entered in from about 2 miles west.

Marsha, Mrs. Roger Yost

Chapter 4

This Tornado's An EF-5!

Sean Wilson, owner of the tornado-chasing service, Blown Away Tours, had started Friday morning with what looked like a normal chase. He and Tim Andrews, who had paid $250 for the tornado show, had left Lee's Summit at 9 a.m. They drove up to Pratt, Kansas, where the air was moist with backing winds, high dew points and a dry line — the division between moist and dry air that is necessary for tornadoes.

It was later in the afternoon when they spotted a supercell near Woodward, Oklahoma, and began to pursue it. It proved to be an impressive storm, but lacked being a tornado, and there wasn't much precipitation. Soon, however, the radar showed that the cell had split, and the part broken off was gaining intensity. It didn't take long to catch up to the rolling storm. Still, with no tornado in sight, Wilson stopped for gas. When he saw three strong rotations on the radar, he began honking the horn, signaling Andrews, who was inside getting a snack, to hurry.

"We need to get rolling!" he urged Andrews as his passenger ran to the car with his snack.

The sky was dark by now. The radar showed they were running parallel to the storm, moving northeast. Around 9:00 p.m., he glanced at the landscape during a lightning flash and saw a small funnel.

"There it is," he yelled, "Tornado on the ground!"

Andrews was seeing his first tornado, and he began to whoop and holler.

With each lightning flash, the tornado got bigger, blacker, 'badder.' Swirling and churning, it evolved into the classic tornado with two smaller satellite tornados circling it.

also said
earlier

Suddenly between two lightning flashes, the tornado tripled in size. Here was the most severe of all storms, the strongest possible, a one-in-ten thousand rarity with sustained wind speeds in excess of 200 miles per hour. This constituted an EF-5 on the Enhanced Fujita scale!

Back at Anthony's, news came that two more homes had been hit along HWY 183 going north, and they might be totally demolished. The grim news started the long search that night for family members: grandparents, children and loved ones. Communication problems soon developed, and it was impossible to get through and hear what was going on.

Over at Don's farm, Eric sent back the report that Anthony was taking Don and his family to Greensburg to the emergency room. Don's vehicles were lying around like broken toys, so he was without a vehicle. He asked his wife Fern to pick him up. She told him she'd try. Eric and the three boys started the two-and-a-half mile walk to the highway in the rain.

Northeast of Greensburg about 15 miles, Brent Unruh watched the ominous, laden sky with a sense of foreboding. He knew, before ever turning his weather radio on, that it would be a bad storm. With this in mind, he began to make preparations. He took an axe to the cellar to chop his way out if he had to. Next, he turned to the propane tank and closed the valve to the house. Lastly, he put new batteries in the flashlight. He didn't know the strength of the storm, yet, but something told him he should prepare for the worst.

He hadn't tuned into the radio in the house for months, but as he switched it on, he instantly heard warnings on several stations. He tried to call his brother Eric, whose farm was just northeast of Greensburg, and in line with the present direction of the storm. Nobody answered. Brent then began trying cell phones.

Finally he reached Eric on his cell phone, who was south of Greensburg, out in the storm, trying to get to Don and Shana's house. Don's new home had been hit, and Don was injured. Debris and downed transmission lines still littered the road, rendering it almost impossible to traverse the roads.

Eric told Brent that some of the farms and homes were already destroyed or badly damaged.

After his phone call with Eric, Brent knew all of his immediate family was safe. Terry and Tamra were in Kentucky, and their parents, Don and Ilene, were in Oklahoma that night. All their homes were in or near the direct line of the tornado, so everything was still a big unknown. He got off the phone and turned on the radio again.

Meanwhile, Titus and his mother, Fern, headed up HWY 183 and arrived at the intersection to Don's farm where they were to pick up Eric and the three boys. They met Anthony in his vehicle with Don and his family, who were trying to get to the Greensburg hospital so Don could get his lacerations stitched up.

"We can't get through to Greensburg," Anthony told them. "I think we'll go on to the Coldwater emergency room." Unbeknown to them, the storm had already taken the hospital in Greensburg.

Eric offered to take Don to Coldwater so Anthony could make sure his parents were okay. Upon reaching Coldwater, Don was taken in to the emergency room to get stitched up, and the boys watched the tornado on the hospital's TV.

Fern, meanwhile, went back to Anthony's with Shana and the children. They still had phone service there. The ladies and children occupied themselves by listening to Carol field phone calls. When there was a lull, Fern tried calling her daughters and the teachers to see if they were okay and their houses were intact, but she couldn't get through. Shana said she thought the school was okay, and two other homes seemed fine. There were emergency vehicles on Aunt Dorothy's yard, however, as her house had been badly hit.

Miss Shayla Kuepfer and Miss Marlysa Koehn had no idea their school term would come to an abrupt halt that Friday, May 4, 2007.

The teachers had been enjoying their new teachers' house for several weeks. At school that day, Miss Kuepfer had a party planned for her students. First, the children would spend half a day studying. Then after lunch, they would have a water fight, and end the day with a snack.

The two teachers had heard about the storm from Tina, which put a little niggling fear into Shayla as she glanced up at the sky. Light, feathery clouds didn't appear too ominous, so she tried to dismiss the thought of severe weather. Should they go to the picnic? They hesitated, but then accepted the invitation, and later were so thankful that they had decided to go.

Over at Anthony's picnic, the evening sky became darker and more threatening. Soon rain, and then hail, sent them all indoors. When the electricity went off, they were among those who headed for the basement. Shayla felt calm among so many people around her. She helped sing with the children to keep them calm.

Feeling uneasy, the two girls decided to go with Renae and Mandi for night. They joined the convoy up HWY 183. They wanted to stop at the house to get their things, but David and Dan told them they couldn't get to the house because the line was down. They also said they didn't know what the house looked like yet, but that Tina's and Lloyd's houses were both gone.

As they drove up the highway they noticed the emergency lights on in the school. That was a good sign, (or so they thought,) so surely the house was fine...

There wasn't much sleep for anyone that night, and the next morning revealed the truth. Greensburg had been hit hard. As they drove the country roads to the school and teacher's house, they wondered what they would find.

When they got there, what a sight met their eyes! The devastation didn't really sink in until Shayla's mom called and wanted to know what it really was like.

Shayla just said, "Terrible".

Many times during the day, Shayla questioned why. Why Greensburg? But, she says, "God had a plan, and still does."

Chapter 5

Protected By An Angel

It was several weeks later. Roger Yost and Lloyd Goossen sat discussing the tornado.

"Yes, some little troubles can be solved with bigger ones," they agreed. By the time both of them had climbed out of their basements the night of May 4, they were no longer worried about hail damage on their roofs.

———◆———

May 4, 2007, began like any other day for Lloyd Goossen. He and his carpentry crew were in the process of remodeling Randy Kelly's house eight miles north of Greensburg. They were planning to remove the living room windows. Mark Dirks happened to be there. He mentioned that the NOAA weather radio was predicting some wild weather, and he wondered whether they should plant Randy's beans. Lloyd told him that the weather channel usually over-rated these storms.

It turned out to be a fairly nice day and they closed up the windows with house wrap and put in a few extra fasteners just in case.

"It sounds like we're in for a wild weekend," Lloyd told his wife, Anita, when he came home from work that night. After supper, he went back out to the shop to work on the counter top he was making for their kitchen. He said he couldn't finish it that night, so he wouldn't be out long. They had added a new living room and garage to their house, and he had just finished new cabinets for the living room and part of the kitchen.

Later, when Lloyd came in from the shop, they listened to the weather radio and heard that a tornado had been spotted around Protection and was headed north. Taking the weather radio and a flashlight, they headed for the basement. Lloyd had his cell phone with him. Anita looked over at the house Tina Berg was renting, and saw it was all dark. 'They must not be home,' she thought.

Anita took the book she was reading with her, and the two relaxed in the office downstairs. Sure, there was a tornado, but Protection was twenty miles away, and most likely it wouldn't amount to anything.

Some friends from Coldwater called to ask if they were in their basement. Lloyd assured him they were. Brandon told him there was a bad storm headed their way.

<hr>

Lloyd's son, Garth, also returned home at the end of the day. With the possibility of electricity going off from bad weather, their three daughters, Kayla, Joni and Heidi were already dressed for bed by 8:30 p.m. After readying some beds in the basement, the girls were ready for the night fifteen minutes later. Garth and Lisa decided to go down with the girls and read for a while so the girls wouldn't be worried, as the weather reports were getting more severe.

Around 9:15 p.m. the rain began to beat upon the house, followed by hail the size of baseballs. As they watched from the basement windows, they saw hail stones bouncing ten to fifteen feet in the air. Meanwhile, the weather radio told of reports of several tornadoes. Suddenly, there was an announcement that a tornado was on the ground in Ashland, heading towards Coldwater.

9:25 p.m.: The hail suddenly stopped, and it became deathly silent. The weather report said there was a large tornado on the ground about 8 miles north of Coldwater, and the areas in immediate danger would be along HWY 183.

The Goossen family decided to move into the pantry, a small room with stairs on one side. There they would have food and drink if anything happened. Sitting on pillows and blankets, they continued reading to the girls so they would remain calm. After a couple of minutes, the power went off, so they read by flashlight.

The wind picked up, and soon they noticed their ears popping. There was a strange feeling in the air.

"I think we should get under the south stairs," Garth said. There would be more protection there. He led the way, followed by the girls and Lisa, all carrying pillows. Tucking the girls under the stairs as far as they could go,

Lisa and Garth crammed in last. The little family huddled together as closely as they could. The noise from the wind was tremendous, and they felt the pressure of it. Loud creaking and groaning from the pressure on the house convinced them the house was caving in.

"Oh, Lord, keep us safe in the storm," Garth prayed out loud. Miraculously, they felt God's presence near them. The girls, huddled together in the back of the stairs, were not afraid; they just felt calm.

After several minutes the noise lessened. It seemed like the wind had gone down a little.

"I'm going upstairs to check the damage," Garth said. Just at that moment, he noticed insulation from the attic in the basement near where they were.

Garth tried to call his parents, Lloyd and Anita, several times to see if they were okay but couldn't get through on the cell phone. Lisa put the girls to bed in the basement. Amazingly, they went right to sleep and slept all night.

The phone was ringing upstairs, so Lisa ran up the stairs to answer it. It was a cousin wondering if they were okay. Garth was standing at the dining room window trying to see through the dark to his parent's house. He tried calling again, this time from the house phone, but it was no use. The phones had quit working.

It was nearing 10:00 p.m., and the weather had calmed down considerably, although it was still windy. Garth told Lisa he was taking the pickup to go see if his parent's place was still on the map. She watched his lights as he drove over there. It seemed that the closer he drove towards their house, the slower he drove. Then she saw his light turn into their driveway and the lights were pointed in the direction of Lloyd's house. She realized then that something had happened, because she shouldn't have been able to see his lights at that point. His pickup stayed parked there for what seemed like an hour, but in reality, it was probably only about ten minutes. She tried calling him on the two-way, but he didn't answer. That is when she started to get scared.

And what had happened at his parent's place? It had started raining and then hailing baseball-sized hailstones. As Lloyd and Anita watched from their south, daylight-basement windows, their son Garth called to see if they had seen the size of the hail.

The weather radio announced there was a tornado eight miles north of Coldwater, traveling up HWY 183. A cold fear gripped their hearts. They knew they were in its path. The wind began to howl. It was time to get into their storm shelter in the northwest corner of the basement, just under a small back porch. Closed in by cement walls on three sides, Lloyd had added extra joists to the floor above to make it safer.

There they stood waiting for... what? The lights were still on at that point. Soon enough, they heard a tremendous banging of objects above them. Dirt sifted down on the water heater across the room.

"There she goes," Lloyd said as they heard the house moving. He crammed Anita into the foot of space between the wall and the bookcase standing against the north wall. He put his arms and hands over and around her to protect her as the banging and crashing became a grinding, grinding, grinding that seemed to last forever. Then there was a big whoosh, the whole floor above them lifted, and they were out in the wind. It felt like they were standing behind a huge jet engine, and it seemed to go on and on and on.

Anita was praying, "Lord help us!" She wondered what would happen next, yet felt calm in her heart.

—◆—

9:31p.m. Lloyd knew they were in trouble when he heard all the air sucking out of the house. The window and exterior-door weather stripping started vibrating and whistling. Then the windows broke out, and the doors started slamming. The noise sounded like a huge turbine winding up as they heard the house disintegrating above them. There was a tremendous banging and crashing, and he could imagine their appliances and furniture swirling around looking for an exit. He felt relatively safe until the floor left, and then he felt very vulnerable. In the middle of all this, something fell on the two of them. It was a ceiling tile from the suspended ceiling in the basement. Lloyd held it right there on their heads.

Finally the wind died down, the grinding and crashing ceased, and they knew the tornado was past. They flipped the tile off their heads, and it fell to the floor.

"I believe the Lord (an angel?) placed that tile over our heads to protect us from all the flying debris," said Anita. Somehow, they felt protected.

After the tornado was gone, and they knew they were okay, they thanked the Lord over and over aloud that they were okay and still had each other. But they wondered about the rest of the family. They prayed they would be okay, too.

Lloyd immediately tried to call 911 to tell the town of Greensburg of what had happened, but there was no answer. He tried to call Garth, and then Roger Yost, but cell phone service was gone, too. Taking his flashlight, Lloyd looked to find the best way out.

"The south basement door is probably the best way out," he said to Anita. The glass, of course, was gone, and the inside door was standing open. It was still very windy as they walked up the slope from the basement. There was a tremendous pile of hay against the south basement wall. Anita asked Lloyd where it came from.

"It comes from our neighbor, Don Edmonston's, hay bales, across the road," he replied.

"The shop's gone!" Lloyd exclaimed as they arrived at the top of the slope. And, indeed, there was only the floor left.

"And Tina's house," Anita added, as she looked again across the yard for the house Tina and her family had lived in.

"I wasn't prepared for the carnage I saw when we went outside," Lloyd said later. He could tell from the noise of the wind and the fact that the house was completely gone that the storm had been horrific, but outside with the light from the constant lightning, they could see electric lines and poles strewn around. All the large cottonwood trees were snapped off at their bases, and the cedar tree windbreak was stripped. There wasn't one salvageable tree on the place. Twenty-eight years of yard work was down the drain in about two minutes.

They looked around them. Large metal feeders had slammed against the basement wall, and a mere twenty feet north of the garage, a truck frame and hoist with dual wheels was lodged. The neighbor's van had landed behind the shop. Never had they seen a tornado do such a complete work of devastation. The garage was a pile of rubble, so they knew that besides losing the house and the woodworking shop, they also had no vehicle.

Lloyd was in his stocking feet, and had no way to get anywhere except on foot. If they walked anywhere, would they find someone to help? Out there in the dark night, with the wind and lightning, it seemed they must be the only two people left in the whole world. It also felt very unsafe, so they went back into the basement and sat under the west stairs on an old coat over some paint cans.

Sitting there, they noticed that the glass in the doors of the bookcase they had been standing beside during the tornado was completely gone. When had that happened? They were inches away from those doors the whole time.

Lloyd kept trying to get Garth on the cell phone but couldn't get through. The weather radio said the weather would be like this until 2:00 a.m. Anita checked her watch with the flashlight. 10:00 p.m. Would they have to sit there for four hours? Would someone come find them? Maybe the police would come! They had no way of knowing then, how busy they were with the town of Greensburg.

And then they heard the most beautiful voice calling from the top of the east wall. "Dad, are you there?" It was Garth! "Oh, thank you, Lord! They must be all right."

Scrambling out from under the stairs, Lloyd hollered back. "Garth, we're here!"

And Garth said, "We are all okay, and our house is okay."

Before they got into his pickup, Anita asked Garth, "When you got here, what did you think?"

"I had no idea if I'd find you, dead or alive. I just stopped and prayed," Garth answered simply.

Chapter 6

Old home place, I'll remember you ...

There it was — the old home place. Many times, Milton had ushered in family members, as well as members of his congregation, with old-fashioned hospitality, a wide grin and an open welcome. Fern, at that time the schoolteacher, fondly recalled when she had been invited to take the soft chair, and Milton had leaned forward in his.

"A fine young man is asking for your hand in marriage, Fern!" the seasoned minister had been delighted to tell her.

The three of them, Milton, his wife, Dorothy, and Fern, had sipped their icy Cokes with delight. Romance and Coke; one warmed and one cooled, and life was good.

This was the JJC Unruh home place. Their service station served the community and a built-in cooler served the growing boys Cokes. Through the years, there was more said about the Cokes and less said about the hard years.

Milton had passed away with a brain tumor four and a half years ago, but Dorothy kept the memories alive and a light in the windows. No one doubted her right to the old home place. She took her round for Unruh gatherings like a 'born Unruh.' Unruh life continued, with the children coming home often.

On the afternoon of May 4, Dorothy's daughter Lisa was struggling with a sewing problem. Dorothy went over to see if she could help. They solved the problem, and then Dorothy stayed and ate supper with the family. Milton and Dorothy's wedding anniversary would have been the next day.

Dorothy planned to go to the teacher's house that evening. The young teachers seemed like family, because they had lived with her for two-thirds of the school year while the new teachers' house was being built. When Lisa made the evening arrangements after school that day, Shayla had replied, "Yes, we'll come, because it's supposed to storm." The teachers were later invited to Anthony's for a picnic, and they had changed their plans.

In the end, it was Rod and wife, Lisa, and their family that spent a quiet evening with their mother, Dorothy. Their young son, Christopher, planned on spending the night with his grandmother. Lisa washed up some fresh, garden lettuce and spinach and then started writing a letter. The last thing written was, "We're under a tornado watch, uh - oh."

"Are you all safely at home and aware of the storm?" Dorothy asked her son, Dan, on the phone.

"Well, Deb and the children have gone to a picnic at Anthony's place, but I stayed home to finish planting a field. I plan on going later." Just then the weather man said that a tornado was sighted around Protection and was heading northeast. Still on the phone, mother and son decided they might be in the path of the tornado.

"But it will probably miss us," they decided. Dan called back and wondered if he should pick her up as she didn't have a basement. She told him Rod and Lisa were there; he needn't worry about her.

They all consoled one another — there was no need to worry about a tornado. Dorothy had weathered many storms in the old house.

Likewise, Rod had weathered many situations too in the past. Once 'Mr. Nace' at Valley View School, he had also been a missionary in Mexico. Patiently he had cared for his father-in-law through his bout with cancer, right to the time of his death. Now he worked with Lloyd Goossen's carpentry crew. Yes, Rod had seen difficult times in his life, so tonight Rod had no fear of a storm.

The children's playing was interrupted when Lisa suddenly called to the children, "It's time to go. It's getting worse outside." It was 9:15pm.

"Christopher, grab your flashlight," she said to her son.

Dorothy asked, "What do I take?"

"Nothing," Lisa replied. "Rod will bring you back." Dorothy took her time switching off lights.

By now it was hailing outside. They all squished into the pick-up, topsy-turvy, Dorothy between Rod and Lisa. Rod's house was only two miles from Dorothy's. As they drove south on the highway and turned west on the school road, the hail increased in size. The continual pounding on the pick-up roof caused Lisa and Dorothy much alarm.

In the seat behind them, the children never made a sound. Halfway there, the hail was so huge and thick that they decided to wheel into Joe Yost's yard and into their open shed.

When the hail let up enough for Rod to drive up to the door, the ladies and Christopher made a dash through the garage into Joe's house. The door was unlocked, but no one was home. Rod drove the pick-up back down to the shed and came dashing in.

They were safely sheltered from the elements, but could never have dreamed what was actually taking place above and around them. Dorothy read a letter she had brought along.

Then the lights were out, and they sat in darkness. There in Joe's dark basement, with no electricity and shattered glass all over the floor from a broken window, they weathered the storm. The phone rang. It was Randy Kelly, an accountant from north of Greensburg.

"It sounds like you're having quite the weather down there," his voice came over the phone. "I'll be down in the morning with my chainsaw." (In Greensburg, about that time, his mother's friends were inviting her to go to the shelter with them, but she declined, "If God wants to take me, He will." She lost her life when the tornado hit Greensburg.)

The wind was howling, and Christopher's ears were popping. They moved to a little hallway. Rod stuffed a towel into the broken window opening. They prayed together and then sat there until it calmed down.

When they climbed the stairs, they were surprised and alarmed to see flashing red and blue lights on the highway over by Dorothy's place. What did it mean? Had something terrible happened? There were some trees uprooted at Joe's place and some windows were broken.

They decided to go check out Rod's place first. Garth was on the road, and he said he was headed for his parent's place to see if it was still intact. (It wasn't.)

Dorothy stayed in the vehicle while Rod and Lisa went in to check out their house. Siding was ripped off both ends of the house. The soffit was hanging askew on the roof line. The roof was intact, but the entire front of the house was pitted with hail marks. Six broken windows and a door, as well as much window screen damage, were visible. The small shed was gone, and the upright freezer in which Rod stored tools was leaning against the mower.

The phone was ringing when they walked in.

"Are you all okay?" Rod's parents from Mississippi were calling. They had heard about the tornado already.

Back on the road again, they met Garth with Lloyd and Anita. They told them that Lloyd's house and new shop, as well as a small rental house where Tina Berg lived, had been totally destroyed.

Awe, terror and dread mingled as they drove on, seeing the devastation everywhere. They saw that the school and new teachers' house were both still standing, although they could see by the lightning that both were severely damaged. Driving further north on the highway toward Dorothy's place, they saw fence posts sheared off at ground level.

Later, Lisa said with conviction, "Even though this tornado may have been time and chance, I do not believe for a minute that it was time and chance that all our lives were spared. It was, without doubt, God's protecting hand sheltering us."

The closer the Nace vehicle drew to Dorothy's house, the more they were filled with fear and dread. What would Dorothy find? Hours before, she had met Tina Berg uptown, and they had discussed the forecast. Tina had wondered if her house would blow away. Dorothy had told her that her house had stood through the storms of many years, and surely it wouldn't blow away. Now she huddled into the corner, hoping, hoping she still had a home.

As their lights illuminated the spot where her house should have been, they saw it was gone! Gone! Dorothy sat huddled in the corner, Lisa's arm around her.

"It's alright, Mom; it's alright," Lisa consoled her mother. But it wasn't all right. Her house was down, crumbled in a heap, and destroyed!

They didn't have the heart to drive on the yard. Slowly, they turned their eyes from the emptiness, worried now whether Dorothy's oldest son, Dan, was okay. On they drove past the unbelievable and shocking scenes of the destruction at the Paul Unruh and Roger Yost homes, and on to Dan's.

Could it be? Again, total destruction met their eyes. It was nearly impossible to even recognize Dan's place! All the many trees were gone; the house, every building, machinery and pick-ups were all wrecked or gone. As they pulled off the highway into the driveway, they were stopped by debris everywhere. Where was Dan? Was he alive? Fear's icy fingers clutched around each of them.

Chapter 7

Tina's Trusting Faith

Tina Berg and her children, Mary and Michael, were at the picnic at Anthony's and were in the convoy that headed north after the storm. They had heard someone's house was flattened along Hwy 183 and hoped it wasn't theirs. Mark's met them as they turned onto the side road, winding past the school.

"There's no use for you to continue on home, Tina. Lloyd's and your houses are both gone!" Mark told her.

"What about Lloyd and Anita?" was Tina's first thought. "And what about our dog? We penned up the chickens and untied the dog before we left for the picnic."

"You might as well come home with us," Mark said. "Well, no ... on second thought, we may not have a house either."

They drove on around the curve and gawked in disbelief. Their home — it was gone, too! All that was left was a bare cement pad with something white sticking up from it. They were glad they hadn't been home to see the house go.

Now they saw lights coming from the west. It was David and Dan. Dan appeared bewildered and afraid.

"Tina, you go up the road to Garth's, and you STAY there!" was Dan's shocked remark. When Tina saw the look on Dan's face, she began to realize how serious this storm had been.

When Tina was a young girl in Mexico, her mother passed away. So as a motherless child, she had moved from home to home working as house help in a German settlement. She wished for a home of her own, and Pete had persuaded her to join him as he headed toward U.S. or Canada. Early one morning, she and Pete slipped under a fence into the good ole' U.S.A. They had been told to try at 7 a.m., because the police were busy changing shifts, and it wouldn't be likely that they would pop over the hill for a border check at that time.

After their successful crossing, they went over rough country through weeds and brush. Eventually, they found Tina's relatives in Oklahoma. Her Uncle Henry welcomed them into his home for as long as they wanted to stay. They stayed there five weeks.

After their child, Mary, was born, Tina started to do some serious thinking. She thought about her eternal destiny. Sometimes she couldn't sleep at night, and Pete would wake up to find her crying.

"Why are you crying?" he'd ask her.

"I'm worried about whether I'd go to hell if I should die," she'd tearfully answer.

"Forget it," Pete would answer brusquely. "You should chase those thoughts away, and live your life and just hope to go to heaven when you die."

No one had ever told her there was a way she could be sure to go to heaven. God must have put that hope in her heart, because she determined to find out, sometime.

Tina had a deep hunger in her heart for God's Word. She received a Bible written half in German and half in English. She so badly wanted to know what Jesus said, that she determined to start at the beginning and read until she found His words. This was very difficult for her, but she persevered.

One day she noticed that she was over half way through the Bible and still had not found words spoken by Jesus. She was taking lessons from a lady on how to read and write, but Tina found it hard to read in the English lesson book. Now when she picked up the Bible, she could read it better and better. This lady got her a Bible that introduced each book, and this helped her to finally find Jesus' words. She remembered reading Matthew 7:7 Ask and it shall be given you; seek, and ye shall find; knock, and it shall be opened unto you: for everyone that asketh receiveth: and he that seeketh findeth; and to him that knocketh it shall be opened.

She had finally found words of Jesus!

"That's just what I'm going to do!" she exclaimed with a deep joy in her heart. "If Jesus said that, I'll do it." She knelt down and claimed Jesus words.

When she left her yard that morning after the tornado, Tina's only earthly belongings fit into a few big garbage bags. She also owned a bedroom suite Mary had lent to the teachers.

Is the tornado the worst thing that has happened in her life? No, she says, the anguish in her heart when she didn't have salvation was worse. There was also a worse time in her life when her son, Michael, was taken from her for awhile. Anything in her life that was not in accordance with God's will was harder than the tornado.

A week after the tornado, Tina had a meeting with a man from FEMA. He said he would have to see the house site to file her claim. She told him she would lead him to the place out in the country. He told her he only knew of damage in Greensburg and didn't believe he would have to go south of town. She assured him she was telling the truth, but he mumbled about being on his way back home to Florida as she continued to drive south.

As she drove past Dan's and Roger's, she tried to call him on his cell phone to see if he believed her now, but his phone was busy. When they reached her place, the FEMA representative made a very sincere apology to her. He had worked hurricane disasters in Florida many times, but had never seen such total destruction before in his life. She told him it was okay; it was quite different than anything she had ever experienced, too.

Rick Schmidt, a life-long resident of Topeka, has been chasing storms since 1977. He has seen over thirty-five tornadoes, including the Hesston, KS tornado of 1990. Usually, he chases storms alone, but he encourages his friends to accompany him whenever they can.

Rick had taken off the week of May 4 to chase storms, hoping something would develop. It looked promising that he'd see some action in western Kansas. One of his chaser friends, Doug, was going out there to chase separately, because of his work schedule. The two of them stayed in contact throughout the day, and Rick stopped in Ness City, KS to wait for something to develop. Doug went on to Kinsley to visit a business client, all the while on stand-by.

By 6:30 p.m., Rick noticed a distant storm to the south of his location. He contacted Doug, and told him where he thought it was. However, from his location, Doug could not see it because of cloud cover. Doug left in his vehicle. Rick followed, but he was sixty miles farther away.

Doug went into Oklahoma to chase the storm. By the time Rick reached the vicinity, there were more storms developing in southern Kansas. Rick, by now, was right in the Greensburg area.

Rick and Doug were keeping in touch but lost cell contact. It wasn't until the tornado was getting close to Greensburg that they regained phone contact.

At 9:00 p.m., Rick got his first visual sighting of the tornado. As he followed it, he met with much debris on the road. Power flashes from snapping power lines created green flashes in the night sky.

"This is a very bad situation," he commented to his friend. "Greensburg is in trouble."

When the wind almost blew his truck off the road, they decided it had become too dangerous to continue following the tornado. They headed into Greensburg to see if they could help.

There was much to do to help the Greensburg residents. Placing their cameras back in the truck, and taking their flashlights instead, they assisted EMT's where they could.

⋙◆⋘

Meanwhile, back on Dan's yard, Dorothy huddled in the corner of the pickup and audibly begged God that Dan would be all right, and that his life had been spared. Lisa, who was trying to find them, was not having success calling on the cell phone.

Slowly, slowly, Rod picked his way over the littered driveway and yard.

"Dan! Dan!" he called. He heard no answer.

Lee stopped by in his pickup. Together the two men searched and called for Dan. Still no answering response.

Dorothy's fear and premonition made her feel like she was suffocating. Her mouth was parched; there was no water.

Rod and Lee had a feeling Dan and Deb were okay, but they still weren't getting any response. Trying to call on the cell phone was futile. Peering into the basement, they couldn't see much of anything. They did hear some banging around, and later found that it was a horse kicking. Dan simply wasn't around.

In their desperation, Rod and Lee knelt down and prayed for Dan and others who may have been in trouble yet. The men sensed the comfort of a literal 'Presence' near them. ("I will never leave thee, nor forsake thee.")

Dorothy's dire thirst continued. Lisa found someone else's water bottle in Lee's pickup. Handing it to her mother, she said, "Here, Mom, just drink it. It doesn't matter whose it is." Dorothy drank deeply, sharing sips with the children.

Finally, Lisa reached Dan's wife, Deb, on the cell phone.

"Is Dan okay?" she asked.

"I think so," Deb answered bleakly. "He was with some storm spotters last I heard from him." But, they wondered, was that before or after the storm?

The women and children sat in the pickup. Outside, Rod and Lee were still calling, "DAN! DAN! DAN!"

Lisa continued trying to find someone who knew Dan's whereabouts. Finally, she reached someone who told her, yes, Dan was okay.

"Thank God!" was her first thought.

After lifting Dan's dazed and drenched dog Abby into the back of the pickup, they drove back to Dorothy's place. This time they turned in the driveway and just sat there, dazed and shocked by all the destruction.

"The garage is gone!" Dorothy exclaimed. "The car is gone!" The round top and all other buildings were gone as well. The familiar old house, the old home place that had been their home for so many years, was a crumpled heap. Oh, could it be true?

The kitchen walls, with a cabinet pushed grotesquely outward, were still standing, plus a few walls. Wires littered the ground. Debris, broken trees, and whatever the tornado had picked up and let crash down again, were everywhere. It was truly hard to comprehend and take it all in. Rod reached into one of the remaining kitchen cupboards and retrieved some things from it. Would the cabinets cave in on him, or would the lines still have power in them? Lisa was afraid.

Nace's family left Dorothy's house, stopping to talk briefly to Dan on the highway.

"I've just come through the worst storm of my life," Dan said. "I took refuge in the basement shower room and prayed to God to spare my life."

Dorothy received news that Tim and Chris, another son and his wife, were starting out from Hiawatha to be with her, driving through the night. The whole situation seemed surreal, nearly unbelievable. Lisa gave her a nightgown, socks and a cosmetic kit containing her immediate needs, perhaps the only things in this world she could call her own.

Kneeling down, the family had a prayer of thanksgiving for lives saved and tried to prepare and settle down for the first of many bad nights to follow.

———◆———

"I can never explain how it feels to have no home to go to," Deb recalled later after the tornado.

May 4, 2007 was a day Dan and Deb would never forget, a day when 'normal life' ended.

Dan was getting ready to strip-till, and they had been working together on the fertilizer pump to get it working. Everything was beautiful and green. Deb was enthused about gardening. The hollyhocks were about to start blooming, and the flower garden under the maple tree was actually looking pretty good in spite of the drought. During the week, she had straightened up the place, cleaned out the north garage and pulled the weeds in the backyard. She was looking forward to having people over for a picnic soon.

"If only I had known," she says with regret, "I wouldn't have had to work so much that week."

Shortly after her children returned from school, Carol called and invited them to a basket-supper picnic. Dan and Deb decided that Deb would take the children to the picnic, so she hurried around and made a casserole, a strawberry pie and buttered a loaf of French bread.

The evening was enjoyable for all. But when the storm blew in, and the electricity went off, it became a confusing and anxious time. Deb went to get her flashlight. Dan called and urged them to all go to the basement because there was a tornado.

Later, Dan called again. "I'm out, Deb, I'm alright, our place is...[static]" Because she was in contact with her husband, Deb wasn't worried.

She was still uncomprehending when he called again, "It's pretty bad, Deb, get set."

"Well, the porch must be gone," she thought.

When her father, Herman Goertzen, called and offered that Dan and Deb could come to their place for the night, she thought, "Well, that's really weird. Why would we need a place for the night?"

The news hit home when Marshal and Carey sought her out on the back porch. "Your place is gone," they told her.

This news was too much for her mind to comprehend, but she followed the first vehicle that left the picnic to go find out what had happened to their home.

Dan wasn't particularly afraid before the storm. Storms had come through their area over the years, but they had never been hit before.

When Deb and the children left for the picnic, Dan left to work in the field. Work was frustrating that evening. Finally, with the storm advancing and the lightning making it too dangerous to stay out any longer, he left for home.

Once at home, he went out to the shed and closed the doors around the Ford pick-up. By this time, tremendous hailstones were pounding the carport roof. Alarmed, he called Deb to tell her there was a tornado coming, then went to the basement and positioned himself in the shower room. There he lost cell phone reception. He believed the noises above him to be hail, and when he felt pressure in his ears, he began praying aloud. He claimed the promise that the Lord would hear if we call on Him.

The noise subsided for a bit, but then began again. The banging and crashing seemed to last ten or fifteen minutes, but in reality it was only two or three. When he was sure it was all over, he tried to get out by way of the stairs. He could not — it was blocked. The window was the only way to get out.

Crawling up out of the basement, he looked down HWY 183 and saw lights coming. "I must get away from this disaster," he thought. Running out to the road, he jumped in with the storm chasers. They tried to contact Deb, but the service was poor.

A gas leak was making a tremendous noise down the road to the south. They drove over power lines and sometimes had to lift them to get underneath.

By now, Dan had reached Deb by cell phone and told her he was okay, but he wanted to see his family. The storm chasers took him to David Unruh's place. Dan and David drove past Lloyd's house, the school and the teacher's house. He reached Dorothy, his mother, on the cell phone and finally arrived at Garth's house. His family was there, and they were all alive. With thankfulness, they knelt down and prayed, praying also for those whom they did not know about.

Chapter 8

If Everything We Had Was Destroyed ...

Krista's happy childhood was marred by one thing: the uneasiness she felt the year she turned twelve. She didn't really understand it, nor could she put it into words.

"I just don't feel happy anymore," she told her mother. It seemed like all her efforts towards happiness and being good just fell into a worthless heap.

One night while out riding in a vehicle, Krista looked up at the stars, and started thinking about the end of time. If Jesus were to come to earth again, would He send her to heaven or hell? Dismissing these thoughts as foolish fears, she decided to talk to her mother instead. Maybe she would reassure her everything was all right.

Krista's mother didn't respond as she had thought. Instead, she told her that she should open her heart to God. She prayed with her that God would help her accept Jesus into her heart when He would call her.

Krista looked forward to revival meetings that year with a mixture of anticipation and apprehension. Would God ask her to give Him her heart? It seemed she was constantly getting into trouble which was making her feel guilty.

The thoughts in her mind kept turning over and over. One evening after church, she talked openly to her parents. They understood the longing in their daughter's heart. How they longed for her to follow God's way!

"Don't ever tell God, 'No,'" her dad said. "That is the worst mistake you can ever make. You can make every other mistake; just don't tell God, 'No'! He wants you to be His child."

One night when she again was troubled by her thoughts, she poured out her heart to God in prayer. "God, I don't know if You are calling me. I don't know if You have given me Your peace. I don't even know if I'm sorry for my sins. But You know! Just give me what You see fit." A light dawned in her heart. She could never be good enough by her own efforts. She needed God's forgiveness and power to be free from sin.

It was with joy and lightness and freedom that she awoke the next morning. She was God's child!

"There is not a friend like Jesus!"

That experience was twelve years ago. Now, as Terrill Yost's young bride, she enjoyed her new life. Roger and Marsha Yost had welcomed her warmly into their family as a daughter-in-law.

One day, shortly before the tornado, Marsha had related a troubling thought to Krista. In their morning devotions, Roger had spoken about Job, and had mentioned, "If everything we had was destroyed ..." The thought lingered. It troubled Terrill's sister, Tara, as well. Remembering how only the previous Sunday, their minister had spoken about this life not being 'heaven,' they had much to think about.

Krista wondered, "How would I react if all our possessions would suddenly be destroyed? If there was a house fire? ... but, no, surely that would not happen!" Uneasily, she wondered if her affections were set too much on her possessions. She remembered a snatch of conversation she had had earlier with Terrill.

"No, Terrill," she had said, "I wouldn't want to do that because it would not be safe."

"Safe!"

Terrill had said it half-teasingly, but his tone also implied, "Who's to say anything is totally safe?"

"Well," she had hesitated, "I guess nowhere on earth is totally safe!"

May 4 was a hot and breezy day. Predictions of thunderstorms with large hail made the young couple uneasy, but that did not keep them from working! So much to do... too little time!

Krista finished planting beans in the garden and put on an early lunch so Terrill could finish planting corn. She spent a busy day. Just before supper, she spoke to her dad on the phone.

"...and Dad," she said, "I didn't put out my peppers or tomatoes yet. I was scared that the hail would beat them up tonight."

"Ahh, yeah, they're calling for hail and tornadoes and all that stuff," her father answered, "but I don't think we'll get it. It doesn't usually happen. I think it would have been fine to plant your tomatoes and peppers."

She hung up and started with her cleaning. A few thunder crashes told her she had better check the sky. Because they lived in a mobile home, they sometimes went to Roger and Marsha's when bad weather was predicted.

She called Terrill to see what he advised. "Do I really need to leave?"

"Well, you never know what will happen,"

"Maybe I'll call folks and get the weather. I'll let you know if I go there."

Then the phone rang. It was her mother-in-law, "There's a tornado watch for Comanche county," she said. "Why don't you come over here?"

Krista decided to play it safe and drive over. Always she had been scared of storms. Kneeling down, she prayed, "Dear God, just keep us safe through this one."

Grabbing some reading material, she jumped in her car and drove the two-and-a-half miles to Roger and Marsha's. She parked the car in the round top, then went into the house and sat at the kitchen table.

Terrill stepped in the door quite a bit sooner than expected. Relief! It was almost 9:00 p.m., and the predicted storm didn't seem to be doing much. They all thought that it may have blown over.

Then... "Ping, Ping, Ping!" Dismayed looks passed over their faces as they realized that the hail had come. Louder and louder it crashed. Their appetites vanished, and they gathered in the screened porch to watch the damage. The garden!...the corn!... the wheat!... the flowers! There was nothing to do, but watch and groan.

Chapter 9

"I Wish Jesus Was Down Here With Us!"

Ryan and RaChelle Unruh had been at 'Grandpa's' [Galen and Linda Unruh] where they had heard about a storm at Protection heading their way. Their two boys, Dylan and Reese, were getting tired, so they decided to go home before the storm got to their area. On the way, the low-fuel light came on, so they drove into town for gas. Ryan noticed how stormy it was to the south and anticipated a rain. Driving south on HWY 183, about five miles from their home, it began to hail. The hail increased in size very rapidly, and with the strengthening wind, the windshield began to crack! Ryan wondered if the side windows would break onto the boys in the back seat.

Within half a mile from home, they decided to turn around and seek shelter in their Uncle Roger's shed. The sheds were locked. (This, they later learned, would save their lives.) There was nowhere on the yard to go. It was hailing too badly to run into the house or open the shed doors. The only place that offered any protection from the hail was a large tree by the road.

Although Ryan was aware that one should never take shelter under a tree in a storm, it seemed the best place at the moment. Parking under the big elm by the mailbox for maybe five minutes, the hail let up just a little, and he attempted continue home. He turned the vehicle back onto the highway. But looking south, an ominous feeling came over him. It was so black! At that moment, the wind began to howl.

What should he do? His decision could mean life or death to his wife and two little boys. He was a man alone with his responsibility in a powerful storm.

Yet he was not alone; he had connected with his God years ago.

When Ryan was a child in Mississippi, he and his two brothers ran free with their two cousins who lived next door. Taking the familiar path through a tree-lined pasture, they would join their dog, Bojangles, in the pond. Sometimes they would head to the draw behind the house, kicking in the dirt to find Indian arrowheads from long ago. On summer evenings, the two families would gather around a picnic table to eat homemade ice cream.

When Ryan turned thirteen, his church held revival meetings. He came home from the first meeting with a heavy burden. At bedtime, he heard his mother come upstairs to visit with his brother; then she came to Ryan's bed side. He told her everything he had done. The next night he confessed his wrongs to his family. He prayed but did not feel much better. He wrote three letters to friends, but nothing changed in his heart. There was one more letter he had to write, a tough one. It was one to his second grade teacher, but when he had sealed that letter, something miraculous took place! He received a sweet peace in his heart, and felt the Lord's forgiveness. He was free! The conversion took ten days, but the change was for a lifetime.

Now as he hesitated in the intensity of the storm, he decided to go back to Uncle Roger's yard and try to get inside the house. Quickly, he drove alongside the back door. RaChelle noticed the bushes twisting in a peculiar way, and thought, "That looks strange."

"How are we going to get inside with this hail?" they wondered. Just at that instant, God provided a "breather." The hail let up just enough for each of them to grab a boy and run. Uncle Roger was holding the door for them and shone the way to the stairs with his flashlight.

The Roger Yost family, together with Ryan and RaChelle and their two little boys, huddled together under the stairs. The awful grating and grinding, yanking and screeching went on and on. The howling wind roared and sucked and shrieked above them. Would it never end?

Under the steps, the little group prayed aloud. "Oh, Lord, we pray for Your protection in this storm!"

Finally, finally, after what seemed an eternity, the wind slowed and the crashing ceased. One by one, they pulled themselves out of their place of refuge. As they emerged, they looked above them. What they saw shocked them! They saw nothing but sky!

"Mommy," a little voice said, "I wish Jesus was down here with us."

"He is, Dylan. He was right here with us keeping us safe through the storm. We just couldn't see Him."

⇒•⇐

Roger's son Chadd's room was in the basement, so he pulled out his shoes for those who were without footwear. A huge tank lay over the storage room which they had been in. It had begun to break through the floor boards above Chadd's bedroom.

Marsha handed one of the little boys up to the men and marveled at how he was trembling in her arms.

They were alive! The little group said a prayer of thankfulness for their safety and asked that He would keep others safe as well.

Roger climbed out of the hole that had been his basement. What he saw shocked him terribly.

"It's gone! The house, the barn, the silo, the bin, the two round-tops, the well house, the farrowing house, the trees... It's all gone!"

The rest of them climbed out of the basement. Destruction was everywhere. They could "feel" it. Because it was dark, they could not see much, but they managed to step over and around the rubble of what minutes before had been the normal, safe, structured lives of Roger and Marsha Yost.

Terrill's horse that was in the corral had a leg missing. Luckily, the boys found a gun and ammunition to put it out of its misery.

The bedraggled group waited by the driveway for a few minutes. A storm chaser stopped by to check on them. The men went with him to see if Roger's other son, Bryce, as well as Galen Nichols' (Marsha's parents) were okay.

Returning to their own home later, Ryan and RaChelle saw with a mixture of guilt and relief, that their house was still standing.

Terrill and Krista's trailer house was also still standing, missed by a mile and a half. The ladies and Dixie, the dog (how did Dixie survive?) drove to Grandparent Nichols' house down the road. The men went back down the basement to salvage Chadd's belongings.

At the Nichols', the ladies sat around the bar in the kitchen. The stark realization of what they'd been through could hardly penetrate.

The men stayed away, and there was no phone service. It seemed dangerous to be out. Everywhere nails and sharp objects littered the ground. What if something caved in? It was dark, and still stormy. The wind was severe enough that one could scarcely stand up in it. Lightning kept flashing... the clock dinged one...vehicle after vehicle drove past... ambulances...police cars.. The clock dinged two...

Krista dozed a bit, but where were the men? She trembled and shook... The clock dinged three... Finally around 4 a.m., they all came back, except for Terrill. When finally he returned, they left for home.

It was violently windy, and they felt unsafe in their trailer house, so they sat in the storm cellar until about five o'clock. Then they went up to listen to the weather. Stormy weather and tornadoes were expected through Sunday. They returned with an air mattress to ride it out until morning.

Chapter 10

Appendicitis! And a Tornado!

"**I** wonder what's wrong with Bryce?" Diane Yost mused to herself on May 3. Her young custom-hay-farmer husband had been complaining about a stomach ache. "Should I stay home from sewing today?" Maybe it was a passing thing...

Well, maybe she would go. She would keep in close contact with him. Scooping up Teghan, her little two-and-a-half year old daughter, and a casserole, she left for church. It wasn't easy to get around any more. Diane was expecting their second baby in less than three weeks.

At sewing, Diane confided in a friend about Bryce's stomach ache, and she seemed more concerned about it than Diane herself. She suggested giving Bryce a call at noon. At noon, she found that Bryce was in no mood to eat, and she told his mother, Marsha, about it.

Later in the afternoon when she returned home, Bryce was in severe pain, and could not even straighten himself. He did not think it was the flu.

"What was it?" Diane called Marsha, who looked it in a medical book.

"It sounds like it could be either appendicitis or gall stones. Call Pratt Clinic," she concluded, "and see what they think."

Pratt Clinic definitely thought he should see a doctor, but could not get him in except for ER. So he made an appointment at Greensburg Clinic, and headed in.

It didn't take long for the doctor to make the diagnosis. "Appendicitis! Get into the hospital at Pratt as quickly as you can. We'll do surgery as soon as you get there."

The next few hours were a blur. Bryce's surgery turned out well even though his appendix had been about to burst. His parents, Roger and Marsha Yost, arrived to take Diane and Teghen out for supper, and then left with Teghen because Bryce would be staying in the hospital for night.

In the morning, Bryce was dismissed with orders not to lift anything over fifteen pounds, nor to drive tractor for a week. Diane wondered how she would keep her husband off the equipment, as this was his busy time.

With Teghan home again, Diane kept busy through the day. True to her predictions, Bryce headed out to the field after he got home.

"Aren't you overdoing it?" she asked with concern.

"Well, the doctor never said anything about not driving swather, just tractor," he answered.

Towards evening, Diane and Teghan took a walk, and they noticed it was becoming stormy. Rod and Lisa, her cousin and his wife, stopped in for some of Diane's fresh garden produce.

"Where y'all going?" questioned Diane.

"To Mom's for the evening," Lisa replied. "Diane, you had better get in out of this weather!" Big drops of rain were splashing down; thunder rumbled threateningly. Bryce drove into the yard with the swather and parked it in the shed. The little family stood at the window watching in amazement as the rain turned into hail — great balls big as a baseball. Never in all her life, had Diane seen such large hailstones! Standing close to the patio door window, she noticed with astonishment that the glass was vibrating with the force of the wind. Bryce was on the phone talking to his parents about the storm.

"Bryce," she said, a bit concerned, "the wind must really be blowing, because the glass is vibrating."

Suddenly he exclaimed, "Mom, the wind has really came up – we've got to get into the basement!"

"Why the snap decision? What made him decide that?" Diane didn't understand.

Bryce grabbed the LED lantern 'just in case,' while Diane grabbed Teghan and followed Bryce down the narrow steps to their little dirt floor basement.

Heavily burdened, she grabbed the nearest seat she could find, which was a recycling bucket. Bryce remained standing. The wind was howling with fury, and the dust was so thick you could bite it.

There was a lull, and Diane asked if it was the eye of the storm. Bryce headed up the stairs with Diane trailing behind. After a quick look around, he ordered her to get back down. They hurried down the stairs again. The wind picked up, and suddenly they heard the loud banging of hail inside the house.

"Oh, no! Did the roof blow off?" Bryce wondered. Or was hail coming down the chimney into the wood stove?

The phone rang. Bryce decided to let it ring. "It's probably Dad calling to see if we're okay," Bryce guessed.

Once the wind calmed down, they went up and Bryce called his parents. After trying repeatedly, and not getting an answer, Bryce became quite worried.

He was looking out the windows. "Diane, you won't believe this!" Trees were uprooted all over the yard, and the recently painted old barn was blown flat. He could not see very well un the darkness,.

"Wow, it must have been really windy!" she thought naively.

"I know I closed the shed doors," Bryce said, "they must have blown open." When it became light enough to see, they saw that the doors had blown completely off. Diane was so sorry that the beautiful redbud tree was reduced to about half its size.

"Don't go outside," Bryce warned, concerned about all the high voltage wires strewn about.

Meanwhile, he was getting very worried that his parents were not answering their phone, and wondered if they were okay. Just then headlights shone on the driveway. It was Roger and Ryan D.

"Are you all okay?" Roger called out. He saw Bryce, Diane and Teghan standing there together, alive and well.

"Our place is totally gone," Roger called back in a sort of hysterical voice.

"And ours probably is, too," Ryan D. added. Diane stepped into the bedroom and called her mother. "Mom, we just had a tornado and Bryce's parent's place is totally gone!" She broke down crying. Imagine! Their place totally blown away!

Bryce went to get the car out of the garage, and they all climbed in. As they were leaving, Grandpa Galen Nichols and neighbor, Don Edmunston, drove into the yard, checking to see if all the neighbors were okay. The little convoy headed up the road, stopping at Dorothy's place. Lee and Karen were there, looking for Dorothy.

"Dorothy!" Lee called into the inky darkness. No answer.

"Rod and Lisa were there for the evening..." Diane offered.

"Oh, no!" Lee shuddered.

They stood in gloomy shock. They decided that all the ladies should go to Galen's house and take, Dixie, the dog. Once there, they sat in stupefied silence. The phone rang and rang, but no one could make a connection. They heard that Dan Unruh was missing, but were very relieved to learn he was safe when the men returned in the wee hours of the morning.

Weary and emotionally drained, Bryce, Diane and Teghan turned toward home. Dirty, yes, but at least a home. It could have been their older house that was blown away. A lot of things one just does not understand.

At the Gregg and Lori Wadel home, Friday began as any another spring day. Their daughter Brooke went off to school, and Lori planned on going to the greenhouse to pick up some flowers with her friend, RaChelle Unruh.

"Maybe we shouldn't plant the flowers today if it's supposed to storm," Lori suggested to RaChelle. But they decided to go ahead, and plant the flowers in pots anyway. Later that evening, she placed the flower pots in the garage just in case it would become stormy, and they all left for a 7:30 p.m. supper at Sheldon's.

Their pleasant evening was interrupted by a phone call from Whitney Nace.

"Get in the basement right away! The tornado sirens have been going in Greensburg for five minutes!"

Hastily they ran downstairs, as the wind began to blow hard. Basement windows blew open. They could hear hail pounding outside. When they thought the storm was over, the men ventured back upstairs. Susan's ears began to pop.

"You better come back down here! My ears are starting to pop!"

The men made a fast retreat back downstairs. Their biggest fear was that their crops would be hailed out. Never would they have believed all the devastation they would soon see.

Chapter 11

Tornado Loose in Town

Lyndon and Denise were looking forward to the weekend. A camping trip was on their agenda, something they had looked forward to ever since they were married three years before.

At lunch when Lyndon came home, he told Denise, "Gregg asked me if I had listened to the weather forecast before planning a camping trip. Apparently the weather doesn't look good."

He called his mother to see if she had heard anything on the weather radio. She told him there was a chance of tornadoes, but Lyndon thought maybe they could go anyways. So, that afternoon Denise started packing their gear.

After arriving at the lake, they started a fire. They would roast wieners while Lyndon fished off the dock. Not many clouds were in sight as he cast into the lake with his new fishing rod, but soon the sky grew darker. Suddenly, it became very windy, and Lyndon's Pennsylvania wife was ready to get out of there! Dousing the fire, they watched a very dark sky and drove through some rain on the way home. Arriving at 410 W. Hancock around 9:10 p.m., they placed their wieners into the oven to broil.

9:23 p.m. They weren't home more than ten minutes when the tornado siren began wailing. But Lyndon wasn't very concerned. The siren had blown before when everything was okay.

"Do you think we should worry about it?" Denise questioned.

"Well, yes, maybe we should," Lyndon responded. He called his mother. Already they had gone to the basement. A tornado had been spotted eight or ten miles from town. Lyndon's house didn't have a basement, so they called their neighbors, the Larry Schmidt's. Larry's invited them over, but they were watching the news and reported that the tornado would miss them by about two miles.

9:30 p.m. Lyndons drove over to Larrys before it really started to rain. Carlene was watching the tornado on the computer, and Larry was following on the TV. The men went out to check the weather and saw large hail at one point. The last time they went out, Larry said he felt the wind make a 180 degree turn!

"We're going to the basement now," Lyndon said. They were in the basement approximately three minutes before it hit.

9:48 p.m. In a corner with three concrete walls around them, Larry sat in a chair, watching to see if the floor joists would hold. Carlene threw a blanket onto Lyndon and Denise and put her head underneath it. Their ears felt as if they would pop. Several times, they felt a rise and fall of pressure. The wind lessened, and then started again. It seemed a L-O-N-G time, but in reality it may have been only two minutes. They heard objects upstairs being thrown around.

Amazingly, during those terrible minutes, Lyndon and Denise both felt quite calm, although Lyndon was worried something heavy would fall on them and the pain that they would feel should that happen. Underneath the blanket, they prayed. Both felt they wanted to be ready to meet the Lord if their time on earth was over.

Finally, the feeling of pressure left, and they knew it was safe to get up. Thankfully, the floor above them held though water dripped through.

Walking up the stairs, they opened the door, and there was the great outdoors. In the back yard on top of the clothesline, a pickup truck sat with its parking lights on.

Lyndon saw it and exclaimed, "There's my pickup! Wait, is that MY pickup?" The white topper was nowhere to be seen, the camping gear on the back was gone, and it was all smashed and bent. It looked like someone had just used his knee and smashed it.

Lyndon started it, but they had to go back downstairs because it started raining again. One of the neighbors came over and said the neighbor's house to the south, the neighbor's trailer to the east, and Lyndon's house were all gone. Lyndon and Denise needed to see it to believe it. Clearing away the debris from Larry's Blazer, all four of them hopped in and went to help others.

Driving first to Larry's neighbors, John and Elsie Unruh, they called for them. John answered they were okay, but needed clothes as they had been in bed when the alarm went off. Elsie told them Johnny's clothes were in the chest of drawers.

Larry said, "I don't think we'll be able to find the chest of drawers because everything has been rearranged!" Denise found wet dresses and a wet shirt. Lyndon threw the items to them, but Johnny wanted jeans! Denise spied coveralls under the debris. They also found one boot. Johnny wore a boot on one foot and went barefoot with the other until the next day when he found the missing mate.

While she was digging for clothes, Denise heard the cries of other neighbors, "Help! Help!" Three men stopped at John's to help push and pull them out of their basement.

Larry and Lyndon continued helping people. Some people were found injured and unconscious, covered with debris. They had no basement for shelter. Instructing others to stay with them, the two men left to find a policeman who called for an ambulance and sent them 'code red' to Dodge City.

Danny and Suleenia Trent had no basement in their home, so they took shelter in their shower stall when the tornado hit. As the wind became rougher, Danny held onto their daughter, Mariah, who was eleven years old. Suddenly, they were flying through the air with the house and then landed with a thud in a gully which ran through their back yard.

Except for her head, most of Suleenia's body was crushed by the bathroom floor. Danny lay in the creek, unconscious but breathing very lightly. Danny's light breathing is what saved him from drowning. Mariah suffered some scratches, but otherwise was okay.

"You need to get this stuff off me, so we can get out of here!" Suleenia told her daughter. Then they noticed Danny wasn't responding, so Suleenia told Mariah to yell and get help for him. Somewhere, Mariah found a flashlight that was not theirs, and started begging for help as hard as she could.

A neighbor, Arlin Wadel, brought others to look at Danny. They were going to leave him as dead, but Arlin did not think it was a good idea.

Speaking to Danny's limp body, he urged him, "You'd better move or something so we know you are alive." There was a slight movement of one of his fingers, and the men tore into action!

A daughter-in-law of Johnny Unruh's had arrived in Greensburg with the Coldwater EMT, and they were on the south end of Greensburg, checking on Johnny's.

When the men discovered that Danny was still alive, they were thankful for the nearby ambulance. He was loaded as quickly as possible, sent to Dodge City, and then later air lifted to Wichita. He had bleeding in his brain, a broken neck, broken ribs, broken back, a punctured lung, a collapsed lung, and dislocated hip. He had no smooth ride in the wind that night!

Suleenia was also suffering severe pain in her back, which was broken in two places. Her neck, too, was broken. She was transferred to Dodge City by ambulance, and then air-lifted to Wichita the next day. Mariah stayed with relatives in Dodge City. She was very afraid her father would die, but miraculously, Danny was back at work five months later, working four-hour days.

Main Street, Greensburg: Total devastation! Buildings were practically unrecognizable. Some people walked, others drove their 'tornado vehicles.' Emergency personnel were everywhere. People were overjoyed to see their neighbors! They were all so thankful to be alive. Rural people drove around checking up on their neighbors and finding out how many had lost their homes.

Much later, when Lyndon and Denise returned to their house, they discovered the west side of the house was GONE! That side had contained the living room, guest bedroom, and the hall. All that was left standing was the kitchen cupboard wall in the middle of the house. Denise could not help but shed a few tears when she saw her china dishes broken in the yard. But all that really mattered that evening was that they were alive, and that they had each other.

A few weeks later, Denise gave a graphic picture of what it feels like to come out of a basement and find out you have lost your earthly possessions. When they had left to take refuge at their neighbors that evening, she had grabbed a magazine to pass the time. Later, although she didn't know why, the more she found that she had lost, the tighter she clung onto that useless magazine. There is something in human nature that wants to possess something for a bit of security. It is hard for us to let go.

Primary tornado with several satellite tornadoes. Looking north prior to tornado crossing Hwy 183. (Photo courtesy of Steve Bluford/Joel Genung)

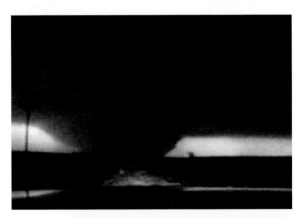

934pm - Tornado beginning to cross Hwy 183 (Photo courtesy of Andy Fischer)

Tornado near Greensburg. (Photo courtesy of Darin Brunin/Dick McGowan)

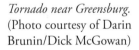

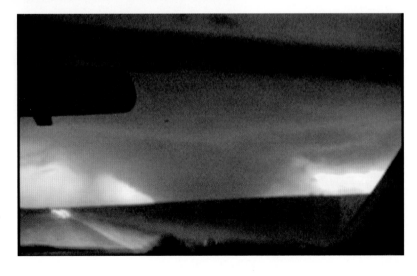

SEVERE WEATHER STATEMENT
NATIONAL WEATHER SERVICE DODGE CITY KS
941 PM CDT FRI MAY 4 2007

...A TORNADO WARNING REMAINS IN EFFECT UNTIL 1000 PM CDT FOR CENTRAL KIOWA COUNTY...

...A TORNADO EMERGENCY FOR GREENSBURG....

AT 937 PM CDT...NATIONAL WEATHER SERVICE METEOROLOGISTS AND STORM SPOTTERS WERE TRACKING A LARGE AND EXTREMELY DANGEROUS TORNADO. THIS TORNADO WAS LOCATED 5 MILES SOUTH OF GREENSBURG...MOVING NORTH AT 20 MPH.

A VIOLENT TORNADO WAS ON A DIRECT PATH FOR PORTIONS OF GREENS-BURG... ESPECIALLY THE EASTERN PORTIONS OF TOWN. TAKE IMMEDIATE TOR-NADO PRECAUTIONS...THIS IS AN EMERGENCY SITUATION FOR GREENSBURG!!

A TORNADO WATCH REMAINS IN EFFECT UNTIL 200 AM CDT SATURDAY MORN-ING FOR SOUTHWESTERN KANSAS.

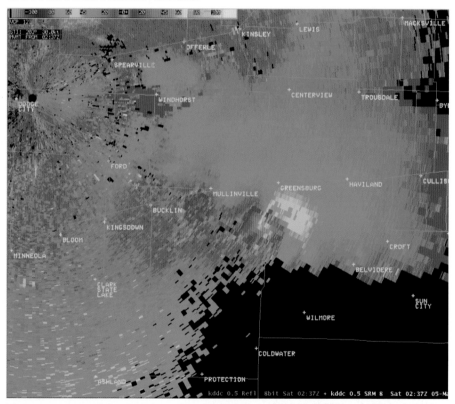

This is an image of the Doppler radar wind velocities in the Greensburg, KS tornado on May 4, 2007. Greens and blues represent winds blowing towards the radar, and reds and pinks represent winds blowing away from the radar. Notice the area to the south and west of Greensburg, where the blue colors (representing high wind velocity towards the radar) are right next to the pink and orange colors (representing high wind velocity away from the radar.) This is a particularly strong instance of what is known as a "couplet" and shows where a mesocyclone has formed in a supercell. (Image courtesy of the National Weather Service Dodge City)

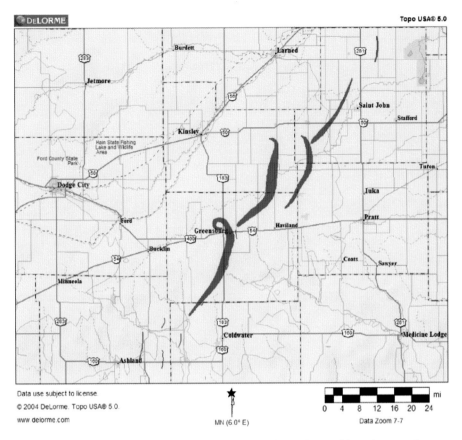

Topo USA® 5.0

Map showing showing tornado tracks for the days of May 4th and May 5th.
(Image courtesy of the National Weather Service Dodge City)

What is an EF5?

It stands for the Enhanced F-scale which rates tornadoes on a scale of 0 – 5. It has been calibrated by engineers and meterorologists across 28 different damage indicators. The old F-scale was supposed to relate the degree of damage to the strength of the wind. The new Enhanced F-scale takes into account the typical strengths and weaknesses of different types of building constructions. This is because the same wind speed will do different things to different types of buildings. An old barn may be blown down much easier than a new barn and an unanchored house will be blown down much easier than a well anchored house. This new Enhanced F-scale should be much more precise and consistent. It will continue to rate the torndo as a whole on the most intense damage within the path.

Residential area west of downtown. (Greg Holmes, thelope.com)

Damage along Highway 54. (Greg Holmes, thelope.com)

Highschool before the tornado. (Wichita Eagle)

Highschool after the tornado. Notice the top floor is missing. (Jeff Hutton, Warning Coordination Meteorologist, National Weather Service Dodge City)

South entrance to the highschool. (Dave Freeman)

The Big Well before the tornado. (Wichita Eagle)

The Big Well after the tornado. (Wichita Eagle)

Drugstore before the tornado. (Wichita Eagle)

Drugstore before the tornado. (Greg Holmes, thelope.com)

Drugstore after the tornado. (Wichita Eagle)

Residential area. West of Main Street. (Dave Freeman)

Greensburg, KS May 16, 2007 - The center of town twelve days after it was hit by the tornado with 200 mph winds. (Greg Henshall / FEMA)

(Wichita Eagle)

Basement filled with debris. This is why you want to be under something sturdy in the basement. (Dave Freeman)

Basement filled with debris. (Dave Freeman)

*New combines at the imple-
ment dealer.*
(Wichita Eagle)

(Wichita Eagle)

*What is left of a late model Blazer or Bronco after
being carried about .75 mile.* (Jeff Hutton,
Warning Coordination Meteorologist, National
Weather Service Dodge City)

*Fire hydrant pulled
out of the ground.*
(Jeff Hutton,
Warning
Coordination
Meteorologist,
National Weather
Service Dodge City)

Years ago, when she was about twenty-one years old, Eunice Wadel moved into an apartment. One night, her brother, Keith, came to share supper with her. Before they ate their meal, Keith said, "God spoke to me, Eunice. He told me that if I was really serious about reforming my life, and living for God again, I should have a prayer before we eat." He prayed then, and asked her if she too wanted to pray. Yes, she wanted to, as well.

Eunice isn't one to waste words, but she says that when she went outside after that prayer, the stars were brighter. The whole world, and her world, had changed. She was at peace with God and promised to live for Him. She has kept that promise faithfully, and God has been there for her through some hard times. Her husband died a painful death, and she has raised her three children carefully, providing for them unselfishly.

Eunice moved into Greensburg after her son Kent and his wife, Stacey, took over the family farm. Following her move into town, she worked at the hospital, and now had recently retired.

On May 4, as the storm was pending, Eunice felt the need to ask God for His protection. Kent was keeping her informed of the storm spotters' reports. His last call was that the tornado siren would be going off. Although no one was living there at the time, he thought she should go to her sister-in-law, Norma's house, because it had a basement. And just as she was talking to him, the siren blew.

9:23 pm. Eunice grabbed her purse and car keys and drove the eight blocks to Norma's house. She stopped behind the garage, ran in to manually open the garage door, and then drove around to the front and parked the car in the garage. She tried to call Kent to tell him she was in the basement, but there was no cell phone service. She sat on the couch in the living room area and waited. It seemed like the siren blew a long time. Then the lights and siren went off. She didn't realize that the city had shut off all the electricity. Now she was in the dark, because she had not thought to bring a flashlight.

As she sat there, the tornado hit. It sounded like the house was going to smash apart. Windows were breaking in the basement, so she groped her way into a room that didn't have any windows. Wind whistled through the house, but she was not afraid. She had prayed, and God was answering that prayer.

After the storm abated, she walked up to the garage. There was glass and water all over, so she went back downstairs, not knowing of the terrible damage that had occurred in town. Soon Kent came to get her and took her to their house on the farm. After awhile, they returned back into town to see if the tornado had taken her house. Most of it was gone!

❧

The John & Elga Unruh home place was tucked alongside Mule Creek near Wilmore, just upstream from a little picnic spot called 'Wade-A-While.' Elga had raised a family of healthy, sun-browned youngsters and from time to time you can still catch a flash of her smile flicker across their faces. Unfortunately, she contracted brain cancer and had passed away.

Years before, John and Elga had made friends with some people from Wichita who would come during hunting season. Over time, these hunters, too had passed away, and their wives had moved to Oklahoma City. Occasionally, John and Elga would look them up to keep up their friendship. When Elga passed away, John was left a lonely man.

Time and circumstance bring about interesting relationships. Elsie Schmidt, a single nurse in the Chickasha, Oklahoma hospital became acquainted with a lady there who was a sister to the two hunter's wives who had moved to Oklahoma City. One day, this patient asked Elsie if she would like to meet an old-time friend of hers, a widower, Mr. John Unruh from Kansas. Elsie replied, "No, but thank you." You see, Elsie did not know if he would have the same faith and that meant a lot to her.

The next time the patient was back in the hospital, she brought up the subject again. And again Elsie declined.

Meanwhile, Elsie's sister Ruby and husband Lewis Unruh wanted John and Elsie to meet, but did not wish to be matchmakers.

Nurse Elsie attended Bethel Home's Annual Gift Day at Montezuma whenever she could. John was a Bethel Home board member, and unbeknownst to both, he had escorted Elsie to her seat that year.

That summer, John attended the annual 4th of July picnic in Dodge City. Lewis and John met at the water fountain in Dodge City Park. "You came here alone last year, and you are still alone," Lewis commented to John.

"It takes two," was John's rejoinder.

John's sisters-in-law had told him about a nurse working in the Oklahoma City hospital, so he asked Lewis about her.

"She is my wife's sister," he said.

John looked Lewis in the eyes, and said, "I'd like to meet her".

This was just the opening Lewis and Ruby were looking for. They wrote Elsie a letter, stating that there was a Mr. John Unruh in Kansas who would like to meet her. Three days later, it occurred to her that this was the same John Unruh her patient had been suggesting. She took the letter to her cousin, Minister Robert at Chickasha. "Should I meet this man?" she asked him.

"Yes."

She told Lewis and Ruby which day would suit to meet at their house. John claims they were both nervous, but Elsie does not remember that part. She remembers what John said on his way out the door that night. "I'm impressed."

The next morning the telephone rang, and it was John. He wondered if Elsie was still there. Lewis answered, "Yes, do you want to talk to her?"

"No, not now," he answered, "I want you to bring her over here for hamburgers tonight."

And that's how John and Elsie found each other. Ruby and Elsie fried the hamburgers, and it was the first of many wonderful meals Elsie would cook for John.

Soon after, John called up Elsie and wondered if she thought her dog, Duke, would like to come live in Kansas.

All this was nineteen years ago. The Chickasha nurse and bride is now an old hand at farming. She gets her share of riding the drills to finish up the seeding, choring cattle, and cooking the kind of meals that go well with Kansas beef. They have lived in their new retirement house in Greensburg for about five years.

———◆———

Friday, May 4 began early as John and Elsie headed south out of town to check cattle. The day was full, so that evening found John and his good wife in bed early. The siren sounded the alarm, and they headed for the basement. They prayed together that the Lord would protect them and all the friends from their church. The Lord honored that prayer. Some of the family called and made sure they were in a safe place, and soon after, the electricity went off, leaving the town in blackness. The siren quit, and in a few minutes the tornado hit. They had debated switching to another bedroom and later were so thankful they had not. Glass and wood began flying around upstairs making a tremendous racket. They pulled the mattress off of the bed and tried to get under it, but the storm was over by then.

It was dark; they had no shoes, and no flashlight. The stairway was full and the fire escape door was jammed. There was no way out. In an hour or so, they began to hear people and vehicles driving by. Soon some men came with flashlights to check on them and pulled them out of the basement over the walls. They were not hurt, and thanked the Lord for His protection. The Lord had directed them to a bedroom in the basement, the only safe room in the house.

They went to their grandson's house and got keys to their son, Mikes house. Mikes were at Hiawatha, KS for the weekend. After trying to sleep, John realized something was wrong with Elsie. He took her to town where they placed her in an ambulance and sent her to Minneola Hospital. She was in shock, and small wonder.

—◈—

Grandma Mae has always loved the children, and children have always loved Grandma Mae. She grew up in a big house with six brothers and five sisters, a close knit family. When they grew too old for spankings, their Dad would admonish them during morning worship, and there was hardly a dry eye when he was done. When the girls were old enough, they ran to the Fairmont store with cream and eggs. As a young girl, Mae also worked for a dairy, washing and filling milk bottles. Allen and Mae were married when she was twenty-one, and they had fifty-eight happy years together. Grandma Mae has been very lonely since her husband, Allen, went to his reward.

—◈—

May 4 was a normal day. She was unconcerned when her daughter, Starla, who lived just around the corner in town, called and said that bad weather was predicted. She was readying for bed when the sirens started blowing and did not let up.

She cleaned some things out of the hall closet and placed a chair for herself in there. Soon, Starla's husband, Jerry, and a friend came and told her that she should come with them to the basement of their house. So Grandma Mae moved again.

Scarcely, had they situated themselves in Jerry's basement when it began to hail. They crowded into the southwest corner of the basement, but rain and hail were coming in through the windows, so they walked through water into another room. A terrible noise started, and Grandma Mae prayed full-time that God would not take anyone unprepared.

After the noise had stopped, the men went to see if they could get out, but the stairway was full of debris. Finally, they cleared it, and what they found when they emerged was a terrible disaster. The van was flipped over. Jerry's pickup had blown over the house. Starla's car had a branch driven right through it. Grandma Mae's house was extremely damaged. The police wanted everyone out of town, so they went to Allen's brother, Gordon and Betty's place. By the time they arrived there it was 3:00 a.m.

⋙◆⋘

9:23 p.m. Christian Disaster Relief work was not a new thing to Robert Koehn. Many marveled how a man over eighty years of age could work as hard as he did. He sometimes told people he didn't have an ache in his body.

Robert and his wife Lois lived near the hospital in Greensburg. Lois was known for her generous gifts of hand-stitched treasures for the home.

It was less than a year now, since Robert had lost Lois, and he was a lonely man. At eighty-four years of age, he was still a strong, hard worker. Recently he and Raymond Wadel were seen working like young men, piling large tree limbs onto a pickup.

Robert and his son, Richard, who is a punctual, steady worker at the county, were visiting that evening when they heard the sirens go off. They went downstairs. After awhile, they debated if maybe the sirens were stuck and that was why they kept on ringing. They decided to stay down there, though, and then they heard some rumbling. The tornado!

When they ascended the stairs after the storm was over, they noticed water coming from the central heating vents. The higher they climbed, the more amazed they were at the damage that had been done by the storm. The house was damaged beyond salvaging.

The apartments across the street from his house were in poor shape. They walked over to check out the county shop, Richard's house, and then on to Ron and Paula's. The town was one big disaster. Lastly, they stopped at Dillon's to report. There they met his daughter, Roberta, and went on home with her, oblivious to the anxious hours his other children would have looking for them. Their vehicles were still at his home, but they were gone.

Robert's son, Marshal, arrived in town with friends at midnight. It took them forty-five minutes to traverse two blocks. Marshal ran to his dad's house, and what a shock he had! It was eerie going through the house, not knowing what he would find. His dad was not there. Finally, after much searching, Robert was finally found at Roberta's house.

A week later, Robert and Richard moved into an apartment in Haviland.

Chapter 12

Memories for Class of '07

The students at Valley View Christian School were understandably shaken when their school incurred heavy damage during the tornado. But they wanted to carry on with graduation and make it a special evening.

Their previous teacher, Marsha Koehn, had moved to Greensburg from Michigan a few years ago. Then she became a permanent member of the community when she married a young man from Greensburg.

Her thoughts were with the graduates, and she wrote some of her memories of the class of '07. This was a special touch to make their disrupted graduation more complete:

"It was the first day of school, the beginning of a new year for four fourth grade boys, and the beginning of many beginnings for a brand new teacher. I was a little nervous, as could be expected, but excited about my new job. I could already tell that I was going to like my students. My first impressions of my fourth graders were that they were all cute, all about the same size, and all big for their age. Later I learned even more things that they had in common. They were intelligent and they loved to talk.

Remember all the many discussions we had? Sometime I could hardly get you to quit talking. One day I told Titus that he could talk at home and not at school so much. He lamented, "Nobody listens to me at home!" Everyone laughed at his seeming self-pity. Later Jesse was going on and on about something and I asked him if he had anyone to talk to at home. He brightened up and said, "Oh yeah, the cats," but then added in a sadder tone, "but they always run away when I start talking!"

Even before the first day of school, I had already been warned several times, "Give those boys a little slack, and they'll take the whole line!" I wasn't sure if those parents really knew what they were talking about. You all were so well-behaved those first few days – quiet, orderly, respectful. But it didn't take many days for me to learn that they certainly did know what they were talking about!

You boys never let things get too boring. I remember one morning watching in surprise as student after student walked in carrying some sort of cell phone – old ones, toy ones. When Jesse swaggered in with an old bag phone, I couldn't figure it out. Later I learned that they "needed" to talk to their friend Alfred, who lived in Antarctica, and had recently slipped off his bathtub and broken his knee. His mother's name was Alfrenia, whom they talked to in a pinch. Fortunately (for me), Alfred died in a few days.

One day I noticed Andy seriously punching numbers on his calculator. I couldn't figure it out because he was working on Language, not Math. The mystery was solved when I saw him hold it up to his ear and carry on a silent phone conversation!

Will you ever forget all the corrections you had to do in Miss Koehn's class? You often would walk in the classroom in the morning and right away look at the chalkboard to see if you had corrections to do and if so, you would try to get them done right away before school started. One morning Andy was busily working away on his corrections and Josh walked in reading Encyclopedia Brown's Book of Amazing Cars. Josh, without hardly even looking up said, "Andy, you just have to listen to this," and promptly read him the whole story of "Desert Ship" while Andy continued to work on his corrections with a slight smile on his face. I wonder if Andy had to correct those corrections!

Then one morning you came to school to find that I had rearranged the desks. Jesse told Josh, "I'm warning you, whoever sits in that place has lots of corrections." Those corrections were a big thing on your minds those days, I believe. I doubt if the change in desks gave Josh many more corrections; he was usually pretty careful with his schoolwork. His papers were so easy to check; I didn't have to puzzle over what he meant, as I had to for some of the others!

Titus was the daydreamer who drew comical pictures in his spare time. A person had to look closely at those pictures, too, or you'd miss a lot of interesting detail. One afternoon when the upper grades were doing a Science experiment, there was a tremendous "BANG" and I looked up in time to see Titus start out of his brown study and nearly come out of his chair. I wondered if he would reveal to his classmates his great scare or opt to just keep quiet about it. I didn't wonder long. Our humble Titus raised his hand and said, "I'm surprised I'm still here and not in space; I jumped so high!"

Andy was usually a cheerful boy, but sometimes he liked to complain a little bit. He'd do anything to get out of doing any more work than he had to. Once he told me that he would give ten dollars for everyone in the class so they all could take one day off of school. "I would, I really would!" he argued. Titus must have shared his views sometimes, too, because he told me that he thought six years of school was enough for him and it was time to give the school management a break.

Jesse would often keep the day from getting too dull by spicing it up with bits of wit. The day the electricity kept blinking, he told us that every time it blinked, it set his electronic brain back to kindergarten, so he was having a hard time getting his work done.

Remember singing in the morning? How many times did we sing one of your favorites, "The Train Song"?! I know it was far more often than I wanted to! Remember the time we were singing it and you all wanted to sing it faster and faster and as a round? You were convinced you could do it and stay together. Well, we started out okay, but we neared the end and everyone was done except group number two, Tristan and Andy. They were singing, loudly and slowly, with completely straight faces. We all looked on in amazement as they slowly finished singing the song right to the end.

We often sang a prayer song at lunchtime. It seemed like you would rather do that than pray. Remember the time, Josh, when it was your turn and we all bowed our heads and you took off humming the pitch? You went up to mi, and then down again and then everything was quiet. I raised my head and asked you what song we were singing and you sheepishly shrugged and said you didn't know! I suppose you were hoping that if you hummed the pitch everyone would automatically begin singing a prayer song! No such luck!

Remember all those games of kick-the-can? Of course, you boys had a hard time playing it the traditional way. I don't know if I'll ever forget the comical sight of you boys lumping your way to the can under cover of the stray tarp you found lying in the yard. Andy was under it one time and there was no way he could see where he was going and he ran right into the swing set. Ouch!

It seemed like a lot of funny things happened in our classroom. Some days were worse than others. Sometimes I think it was just the mood everyone was in and stuff seemed funny, and it really wasn't that funny. Sometimes I'd get on your case about laughing too much. One day, I really got on your case and was quite stern with you. Almost right after my sobering talk, Andy came up to my desk with a question. On the way, he stumbled a bit and his Math book went flying out of his hand and went crashing into the wall. Papers were scattered. Andy frantically grabbed at the papers, while looking at me out of the corner of his eye with this worried expression that I interpreted to mean, "What is this grouchy teacher going to do to me? I didn't mean to do this!"

I knew it was an accident, so I returned to my work, while Andy got his papers and book gathered together. The room was deathly quiet. I was quite pleased, because only minutes before, such an incident would have had the class in gales of laughter. I was sitting there so proud of you all when I heard it — coming from somewhere, out of that quietness —one short stifled snort. That snort did it. I blew it. The whole scene struck my funny bone and I laughed. And I couldn't stop. So of course, the whole class erupted into merriment, just as I had strictly forbidden them to do only minutes before. It was really my fault, but I sent the whole class out to do laps around the school, more to run off energy than for punishment!

Remember all the good times we had — going down to the pasture for devotions, to the cottonwoods for story time, field trips, singing, and, yes, all those "discussions?"

I have many fond memories of those two years teaching you boys. Thank-you for making them two years of good memories.

Wishing each one of you much happiness in life,

Marsha Yost – (or as I was then known — Miss Koehn)

Chapter 13

"At Least We're All Alive!"

Now, nearly three years after those carefree school teaching days, we find Marsha happily married to Aaron, and enjoying their baby, William.

It was starting to get stormy that Friday evening at the Aaron Yost home, so they listened to the weather monitor to see what was going on. A tornado watch was announced for the area, so they kept listening for further updates.

As the warnings started to come, Marsha told Aaron about them, and how she was nervous. He didn't seem too concerned, so she decided to give William a bath before things got too serious.

9:23 pm. It was after a quick bath, while she was dressing the baby that the tornado siren went off. They headed for the basement and she finished dressing him there.

Aaron kept dashing upstairs to get cash, diapers, clothes, etc. He plugged the monitor in at the top of the stairs. It was getting so stormy that he would have to dash to the top of the stairs to listen to the monitor. This all made Marsha uneasy, and she found herself wishing he'd stay in the basement! Neither Aaron nor his brother Craig in North Carolina could reach their parents, Joe Yost's, on the phone. Finally, however, they reached them and learned that they were at Joe's parents, Harlin and Jean Yost, waiting out the storm.

After another quick dash up the stairs to listen to the weather monitor, Aaron came back down and told Marsha that it said the tornado was six miles south of Greensburg on HWY 183. He quit listening then and started praying for people in the path of the tornado.

The electricity went off shortly after that, and with it, the siren. Aaron's brother, Craig called again. It was very stormy, so Aaron cut him off with, "I have to get in the bathroom, the tornado is about to hit!"

———◆———

Joe and Karen Yost live down near the school, and had been taking care of their grandchildren, Craig and Tanya's twins. They had just taken them over to the Tim Nace home earlier that evening.

Joe was born and raised in the community. In a quiet way, he has for many years been filling positions of service. We are often inspired by his encouragements.

It was getting stormy, but they continued to visit at the Nace's for a bit. By the time they left, lightning illuminated the night sky. Going into the town of Greensburg, the storm seemed to worsen, and they decided to go to Joe's parents, Harlin and Jean Yost. By the time they arrived, the lightning was incessant. They had just dashed in when the siren began wailing continuously. Joe tuned in Harlin's scanner, and they heard all the activity, which was very scary.

Joe heard the emergency vehicles were starting out for Greensburg even before the town was hit. This worried them about their farm, as it sounded like that was where the tornado was. Karen donned one of Harlin's sweatshirts for her nervous chills and went down the cellar so she would not hear the scanner. Craig called from Grifton, NC to warn them about a tornado on the ground.

———◆———

Craig and Tanya had been together with friends that evening, playing softball and feasting on BBQ wings for supper. After tucking their four-year-old daughter, Madison, into bed, they began to pack for the return flight in the morning. A few minutes after ten o'clock, Craig's cell phone rang. It was a business man from Ashland, and knowing they did not have TV, he was worried about Joe and Karen. He wondered if they knew there was a tornado on the ground headed for their place. Craig thanked him for calling and immediately began to call his parents.

Immediately, a terrible fear gripped Tanya, because she knew their twins, Ethan and Elle, had spent the day with Joe's. On the other hand, Kansas has many tornadoes, most of them barely touching down, maybe only knocking over an old barn, tearing out fence, giving the storm spotters a bit of excitement and then dissipating.

Next they called Tim's to see if the twins were there, who reported that Joe's had recently dropped them off and were headed for town. Craig then called Aaron, his brother, who lived a few blocks from Grandpa Yost's and had not yet heard about the tornado. As they were on the phone, the sirens started going off in town...

———◆———

At Grandpa Yost's in town, a couple of chairs were moved to the cellar and Grandma Jean was helped down stairs. The storm cellar boasted a concrete top to make it a safer place. The ladies were seated in the cellar when Aaron called. Suddenly the power died and with it the noise of the siren. Joe told Harlin that he should go down the cellar. Harlin would have preferred to remain upstairs and see what would happen, but finally both went down. The noise of the big hail slowly died away and all was quiet.

9:44 pm It was then their ears began to pop, and the wind began blowing hard. The house started breaking up, and the grim reality struck when parts of the house crashed down the cellar stairway. They realized the house had given up to the 205 miles-an-hour winds. It was terrible! Bang! Crash! Smash! with the wind roaring and plaster and debris raining down the steps. The door at the top of the cellar stairs blew off, rain poured in and they were soon standing in water.

By this time they were all praying aloud. Finally they could tell the wind was lessening and Joe went up to devastation! He was so anxious about Aaron's that he ran the three blocks. Harlin, Jean and Karen waited in the cellar.

Harlin and Karen began to pick their way out through the debris. It was still raining with the wind blowing hard. Outside, flashlights bobbed along, and people were calling out names into the darkness. It looked like a war zone. Jean was nearly in shock, so Harlin picked his way into their downed house and brought back his heavy winter coat with a fur collar.

He kept saying cheerfully, "Jeanie, at least we're all alive!"

Karen was so very worried about Aaron's, Craigs' twins and numerous others. Finally, they heard Joe and Aaron's shouts who were back to help Jean out. They had to crawl over the downed garage roof, but they all made it. Joe and Aaron kicked out the remainder of the pickup windows and crawled into the pickup and it started! They cleared out some of the debris behind it, and Aaron tried to back out. It hooked onto the other pickup, but Joe encouraged him to "Just try gunning it more." (It was so uncharacteristic of these responsible Yosts to ignore the damage 'more gunning' could do. They must have thought that things were beat up enough, a little more didn't make any difference.) So Aaron 'gunned' the motor and was able to back out.

———◆◆———

Back in Aaron and Marsha's basement, Aaron joined Marsha and William in the bathroom. Soon their ears were popping and Aaron closed the door. Marsha huddled over William, who was awake and perfectly content in her arms. Aaron huddled over them both and began praying.

Insulation blew in, and the door rattled back and forth. It grew extremely windy and they heard things crashing, banging and breaking. Finally the loud noises quit, and lifting their heads, they walked out of the bathroom into a very dirty basement.

Aaron climbed the stairs and looked around and went back down to tell Marsha that the house was still standing. They didn't know what to expect; there had been so much noise!

The storm finally passed by and Aaron left to check on his Grandpas and parents. He was turned back by high water in the streets and returned for his boots. He checked in on their elderly neighbor, Ed Pooler, and just as he was leaving, Joe showed up at the door to see if they were okay. Aaron asked if they had a dry place to stay, and he said, "No." So Aaron left with Joe to get the rest all over to something dry at Aaron's place. They returned in the very smashed pickup.

After settling them onto a dry mattress in the basement, Joe and Aaron left for south of town to see what was left of Joe's place. They had no idea what they would see. A long time later, they returned in a different pickup with the good news they could all go out to the farm! The family was relieved to have a place to go, yet saddened when they learned of others who had lost their homes.

The ride out to Joe's seemed a nightmare — the dark night, debris everywhere, homes destroyed, the hissing, leaking gas line, utility poles on the road, and the worst - homes that were GONE! They were so thankful when they finally reached Joe and Karen's house around 2:00 a.m., glad for a dry, safe place to spend the rest of the night.

Aaron and Marsha were so thankful they escaped without any bodily harm, and all their friends were also alive and well.

As Joe and Aaron headed out to the farm, their trip home was surreal, and they were stunned by the devastation. Joe felt like stopping to check on Dans, Rogers, Pauls, Dorothys, Tinas, and Lloyds, yet knew they must continue on to their place to see if there was any damage there. Joe feared to see it, but knew he must.

Imagine his relief when he saw everything was still there! The house and warehouse were damaged, but standing. They could not linger long, as they needed to get back to Greensburg to "rescue" Karen, Marsha, William, and Harlins.

As they headed back to Greensburg to get the family, they saw fence posts between their house and Lloyd's sheared off at ground level, and there just isn't anything much tougher than an old hedge post. They maneuvered their way back into Greensburg to get their loved ones who would live with them for the next week. They were thankful to be alive, but the enormity of it all just didn't sink in at that point. They drove back to their house and finally went to bed at 4:30 a.m.

Chapter 14

"We may be in for some trouble this time ..."

In the fall of 2006, Curtis Unruh remembers pondering several times whether there wasn't something in store for the area someday. He read about Florida being hammered so badly by storms, and then New Orleans. He wondered if it were possible that lives here in Kansas would be changed.

Curtis is a member of the MUA committee for our church, and it just so happened that it was time for people to re-evaluate their Aid plan. Today he had calls for cancellations or for more coverage. As he answered phone calls regarding changes in their aid plans, the weather radio kept hammering out warnings about storms, serious storms. He heard that there might be storms and possibly severe ones.

A few days before, Curtis had been showing his son, Wendell, some things that his late wife, Ruth, had saved for the children and grandchildren. (Ruth had passed away three years before.) Now since the tornado, he wonders where various items went in the storm. He did not think those things meant much to him — the jelly dishes found in the old house his folks moved into when they moved to Greensburg, the butter mold with a note written in his mother's handwriting, saying it had come from her grandmother and the china cabinet his Dad bought for his mother, hauled home on top of a load of barley, which she in turn had sold to Ruth. He wanted the children to know the history of these things; now he wonders why he didn't give them instead of only telling them about them. Now they all are gone.

9:23 pm. A year ago Curtis found another companion, Joann, and on the night of the tornado, she was relaxing in the recliner while he sat at the kitchen table busy with MUA bookkeeping. When the storm sirens began to scream, Joann really didn't think anything would happen. She and Curtis went downstairs, leaving the MUA papers on the kitchen table.

Downstairs, they decided on the southwest room. Curtis moved some chairs into the room, checked a small flashlight he had down there and then decided just in case they needed a bigger flashlight, now might be the time to get one. He went upstairs to the garage and retrieved one from the back seat of the car. Again he walked right past the MUA papers and back downstairs to listen to that never-ending siren.

"We may be in for some trouble this time," warned Curtis. He thought they should have a prayer for their safety and also for their friends, so he prayed in his thoughts. He wondered later why he didn't suggest getting down on their knees and praying, but he did not want to scare Joann unneccesarily.

Finally the siren silenced, and the electricity blacked out. The phone rang incessantly as Curtis' sons kept them informed. Dwight told them the storm was at least a half-mile wide. They could see the dust behind the storm and estimated it to be six miles north of the county line, and over to the west, right in line with Don Koehn's place.

Outside, the weather was miserable. Rain, hail and strong winds lashed at the house. Something began pelting against the house — what? Things were cracking; glass was crashing down. Water dripped in the basement and ceiling tile fell down in clumps. Things fell on the stairs that Joann knew belonged in the back and spare bedrooms. Suddenly, the barrage of noise intensified, and they felt a little draft of cool air.

"We've just lost our home," Curtis informed Joann. They shone the flashlight up the stairs and there were boards, sheet rock and plywood blocking the way out. They would need to wait until someone cleared a way for them. Joann wanted to get right out of the basement, but Curtis told her it was raining out doors.

"We are better off right here for now," he assured her. He thanked God that they were unharmed.

After waiting for help, several neighbors stopped by to help them out of the basement. Joann had no shoes on, so they asked what size she wore and one of the neighbors got her a pair. The men took Joann across the street to a neighbor's house, and Curtis went to see if the neighbors were all okay. He could not get to his sister, Sharon and Bill Sutton, so he came back.

Suddenly they heard a lot of noise behind what had been their house. It was Dwight and Tammy and their children trying to get into the basement to see if they were okay. Curtis told them where Joann was and asked them if they had been by any motels. He thought they needed a place to stay.

It was then that they realized that the whole town, or most of it, was gone. Comanche and Barber County fire trucks were all over their part of town already. The fire trucks had followed the storm up from the south. Curtis asked one of the drivers to check on Aaron's. They went immediately and also checked on Ralph Schmidt. Ralph was okay, but wanted to know about his wife, Lillian, who was in the hospital. They told him they had not heard of any casualties.

Chapter 15

A Scene Like Out Of
A Horror Film

Over at the National Weather Service office in Dodge City, Mike U. had a night he will never forget. At 3:00 a.m. he was still stirred up. He should have been going to bed, but he just could not. His mind was running overtime on what he had just witnessed.

The storm of the day erupted at the southernmost end of a cluster of pseudo-organized right and left members to its immediate north. But the far southern storm that erupted out of nowhere just had that shape. Not two minutes after he issued SVR again for eastern Clark Co for that storm he issued TOR...and he did not have to wait for strong 0.5 convergence/couplet. It took awhile to get going...about Protection or so... but when it did it went on to produce a fantastic velocity signature 0.5/0.9 slices north of Protection. The couplet was tracking more northeast... missing Coldwater to the northwest and approaching Highway 183 about seven miles south-southwest of Greensburg. Velocity rotational couplets were topping out at around 150 knots total shear over about a half mile radius.

He was just thanking the Lord that it appeared to be missing Greensburg to the southeast. The next couple slices, though, frightened him. The couplet was bending to the left...and he didn't even really give it thought...the "...tornado emergency for Greensburg..." in his next SVS... was like instinct – he just did it. Those few minutes after watching one of the most incredible velocity couplets go directly over a good sized community in his CWA...he was just too anxious. Then the message was sent out...a plea from Greensburg dispatch... "Ford County communications this is Greensburg...we just took a direct hit..." that came no more than about three or four minutes after the couplet passed over, he then immediately sent out another SVS indicating that Greensburg likely took a direct hit.

Thereafter the steady-state cycling of tornado cyclone tornado...left turn... next cycle...tornado, left (north) turn...next cycle...it was routine...the most steady-state cyclic significant tornadic supercell he had ever seen, let alone work the warnings on radar. He didn't think that there was one minute from the time of the first tornado near Protection to the time it exited his SWA and headed into the Ellinwood area, when there wasn't a significant tornado tearing up things over that hundred mile stretch.

One hundred miles of steady-state tornado production! Mike's not sure how many members there were in this wedge-family. Just to see hours on end of velocity signatures like this was something he will never forget. Inbounds of 120 knots and higher at times...inbounds only! One would expect to see this only several times throughout a lifetime! He thought the highest they had ever seen was about 150 knots that actually looked like legitimate data (as in properly aliased).

Greensburg was pretty much gone, especially the western half of the town by what they could surmise from the media reports and interviews after. The tall tower that once proudly stood above the Largest Hand-dug Well was no more. Completely gone! The Big Well was located in the heart of town.

When the storm chasers drove into Greensburg, it seemed like they were walking into another world.

People walking down the middle of the highway waved them down for a ride. Dick told them he could take three at the most, but that they could come back for more if needed. They let an old man rest in their car, and took two Mexicans into town and came upon a horrific sight. It was like a scene out of a horror film.

Dick, Darin and Derek walked about, completely in shock. It seemed like a dream, like something that you are actually seeing, but knew it could not be real. It was almost as if the mind was refusing to believe what it saw. Along with three or four other people, they were the first to arrive. People were walking around like zombies, unmindful of what had just happened.

They talked with these people, offering what they could and trying to make sure that everyone was okay. They watched twenty survivors who had been hiding in a convenience store freezer, come walking out. They filmed that shortly before putting the camera away.

At about this time, emergency vehicles started pouring in and it was good to see that help was on the way. After thirty or forty-five minutes, they organized a search team, and walked down a street where there were no rescuers. Going from house to house with no flashlights, they used their cell phones as light, yelling "Hello" into basements in their search for people. You can't imagine what it is like to do this over and over. Dick had never seen a dead body, and was terrified of the sight of blood, but he kept walking. They never did find anyone.

The three men continued on to the east side of town, talking with people, making sure everyone was okay. They rendezvoused with MESO (a group of storm chasers) for a bit, and then headed back to the car. Everyone was meeting at Dillon's for a body count, to determine who was accounted for and who was not. They continued to talk to other people, and some of them asked if they had seen so and so, or their dog, or if they knew if a certain house had been hit. Some tried to use their cell phones, but the cell phones quit working shortly after they arrived.

Walking back into town, they decided there were enough emergency personnel there to handle things. They didn't want to get in the way, or be a burden. When they left at about 1:30 a.m., they realized three-and-a-half hours had passed. No motels were available so they had to go back to Wichita, meeting about three hundred vehicles heading into Greensburg from elsewhere.

The smell of Greensburg that night has stayed with Dick. Words can't even describe what the smell was like, maybe more of what the smell made them feel like. Terror. Death. Chaos. Delirium. All of these wrapped up into their minds and emotions at once.

When they got back to Wichita, Dick couldn't sleep, and then later he slept all the time. He felt guilty that he couldn't do more to help those people that night. Darin and Derek were feeling the same way.

It is a miracle that more people weren't killed. There was perfect coordination between chasers/spotters and the National Weather Service and the media (especially KAKE in Wichita) of relaying reports with precise information. It couldn't have run more smoothly. With the issuance of the tornado emergency for the city of Greensburg, and the distribution of this wording via KAKE and other stations in Wichita, it definitely saved many, many lives.

Storm chasers Sean Wilson and Tim Andrews put their cameras aside and started clawing their way through the rubble to uncover people crying for help. Hearing a cry under a pile of rubble, they started to pull away pieces of house, roof, furniture and tree limbs and got a hole big enough for a woman to stick out her hand. Sean clasped it gently.

"Are you okay?" he asked.

"I don't know," was the reply from down in the debris. "Please hurry." The lady survived because she had taken refuge in the bathtub in her basement bathroom.

Then he met a woman, holding a dog and walking down the middle of the street. She had a blank look on her face. He pulled up and asked her, "Are you okay? Are you hurt?"

"I don't think so," she said. He let her into the back of his SUV. She had been driving through Greensburg, pulling a trailer full of horses. As the storm descended on them, she was among those who took shelter in the freezer of the convenience store with twenty others. The twisted metal, once a freezer, was in two pieces. Her truck was gone, but the horses had survived.

After a night of that, Wilson was exhausted. Saying a prayer, he headed back home. Calling his wife from the road, Wilson broke down and wept.

When Autume Wadel got off work at the courthouse, she took a walk, and then dropped in at her grandparent's house, Ray and Neoma Wadel, to do some sewing. She had agreed to teach school at Hillsboro, KS the coming school term, and was working on her wardrobe for that.

It seemed like any other night, but they would have never imagined how long the night would be. Later in the evening her mom called and told her it was raining in Bucklin. She called back a little bit later to warn her not to come back into town without calling before she left, because she had heard storms around Ashland were moving that way. Not too long after her phone call, the electricity went off, and the wind, rain and hail started picking up outside. More family phone calls encouraged them to go to the cellar, so they headed down to the cellar.

They all settled down on their folding chairs, waiting for whatever was to come. Outside they could hear the wind getting stronger, and it sounded like the hail was getting bigger. After a little bit it got quieter and they went upstairs to check things out.

Autume decided to call her mom and see what the storm had done in town. She said the storm hadn't arrived yet, but was coming and she had to go for shelter. Autume waited awhile before trying her again, but got no answer. About this time Dan Unruh drove up and asked if everyone was alright. He said his place and his mother's place had been hit.

The phone service was poor, but she kept trying to reach her parents and finally got through to her Aunt Susan. She said town had been hit, but she didn't know how badly. After Autume heard that Greensburg had been hit, she again tried to get her parents on their cell phones, with no success. About 11:00 p.m. she reached her brother Zane in Lee Summit, MO, on the phone. He had heard about the tornado and was getting together with her other brother, Alex, from Manhattan, KS, and they were leaving for Greensburg. They had not been able to communicate with their parents yet either. Awhile later Zane called back and said their parents, and sister, ShaRae, were all okay.

Autume and her grandparents sat around and tried to comprehend what had happened. Outside the sky was still flashing with lightning. You could not hear thunder, and it looked like someone was flipping the light switch on and off. The phone rang on and off and it seemed rather strange that no one really had a concept of what time it was or how late it was. They all just seemed to know that no one would be able to sleep after all that had happened. They decided to try and get some sleep anyway.

Around 3:00 a.m. they heard Arlin's pickup coming up the driveway. Autume's parents, Arlin and Shelly, and sister, ShaRae, and their dog came into the house. The family sat in the living room, talking about the devastation of Greensburg. They again tried to get some sleep, and when they got up a few hours later, the boys were just arriving. They had to go all the way around Greensburg to get there.

———◆———

Mr. Richard J. Fry, 62, from Albuquerque, N.M. was on his way through when the storm hit. He was found later in the Greensburg Lake. Divers were brought in from Wichita. They found his pickup in the lake as well.

———◆———

Sarah Tackett, 72, lived alone in Greensburg with her very shy cat. Because she was kind to it, the cat trusted her. When others came in the house, the cat would find refuge under Sarah's chair. Sarah didn't live through the tornado and we wonder what happened to her cat?

———◆———

At the Jayhawk Motel, Lois Morehead was moving all guests, off-the-road travelers, and residents to shelter. She was trying to lock the front door when the manager's son, Jerry Deimert, drove in to take cover. She asked him to help her hold the door as the wind was getting too strong to fight. They were too late to take cover, and when the tornado hit, they were blown to the floor.

———◆———

Stan and Dolly Adolph, and their daughter, Debbie, with her little ones, Alec and Alexas, were imploring God's protection while the tornado tore up their house. Their dog, Bentley, was in a pet porter down there, also, howling and barking.

When it was over, the dog was quiet and the children started crying. They were sure the dog was dead. They went over and let him out of the pet porter, and he was as glad as they were to be alive.

Unable to get out, they prayed again for God to help them. Dolly said over and over, "God be with us, God be with us." And indeed He was. Hands reached down and started pulling them to safety. Dolly said those hands were a young man who said, "I'm your neighbor". She said they didn't have a neighbor like him, and when they turned around to thank him, he had vanished. They thank God for answering their prayers.

Chapter 16

Awe at God's Great Power

Across the town of fourteen hundred people, nearly a thousand homes exploded. The first rescuers were fellow neighbors. The professionals rushed in from surrounding towns, but depended heavily on the people of Greensburg in the first hours after the tornado went through.

During the siren, Chris Wirth, one of the bankers, hurried down to the bank to switch the computers off. As he drove back through the streets, he realized there was too much debris flying around to get out of his pickup. Something hit the right hand side and knocked the window out. An airborne tree fell onto his pickup bed. As he sat there, he saw a twenty-foot tall tree uprooted right beside him. When the storm calmed a little, he went to check on his neighbor. It took him three hours to get that neighbor out of his basement. Thankfully, both were unharmed.

Lists of the residents evacuated were made, but some of the residents fled before the tornado, and others left before checkpoints went up, making the accounting difficult.

———◦———

As soon as the air cleared, Tim and Sandy Nace headed for town to make sure some friends were okay. They turned down Main Street and couldn't get past the vehicles of people already looking for loved ones. Jon, their son, started clearing streets by the rodeo grounds with the backhoe, but the trees were too big to handle, so Jon went back around Main and worked on moving poles there.

Tim and Sandy pulled a vehicle out of the mud. (These people were desperate enough to try driving in the field to get where they needed to go.) At that point, Tim didn't realize the immensity of the devastation. It was dark and they were trying to get to Harlin Yost's house, and trying to check on another friend close by. They cleared the road with the backhoe as they went up Main Street near the high school. Lights were on at Harlins, so they knew Harlins had been in the cellar. Their other friend was sitting asleep in a chair among the debris. He'd had back surgery, and was medicated, but coherent enough to tell them he had been in the neighbor's basement during the storm.

Ryan Penner and Marshal Koehn came running by, wondering if Robert and Richard had been seen. They took the backhoe to Robert's again, and started digging. However, they couldn't find anyone, and learned later that Robert and Richard had been seen walking to the county shop after the tornado. They all went home at 3:30 a.m., assured that as far as they knew, no one was missing.

—◆◆◆—

As Brent Unruh tuned into the weather again, he heard that it looked like Greensburg took a direct hit and the tornado was moving northeast through the city. That was coming in his direction at about 10:15 p.m. He soon lost his electricity and the wind started coming up. He walked out on the enclosed porch, trying to decide what to do next.

"The Lord hath his way in the whirlwind and in the storm, and the clouds are the dust of his feet." Nahum 1:3.

"I would hasten my escape from the windy storm and tempest." Psalm 55:11

Brent walked down to the cellar. Overhead, the storm raged. He felt uncertain, but then came to the conclusion that everything was calm again except for the lightning and rain. He emerged from the cellar.

The first storm that sent him to the cellar had passed about three and a half miles west of him, leveling his neighbors' farms and everything in its path. But a second storm was raging southeast of him now and it was more frightening. He could hear this one, and it sounded like they say they do – a freight train! It was calm at his place then, and he could distinctly hear the storm that was passing by just a little over a mile east of him. Then the wind began to come up and muffled out the distant roar of the storm. This put him in the cellar again for a few minutes until things had settled down again.

The next morning he found out this second tornado east of him had been just as powerful but not as wide as the one that touched down west of him earlier. It was about a half mile wide and had killed one of his neighbors to the northeast. In the light of day, he found he had been wedged in between two powerful storms that destroyed many farms and trees on both sides of him.

But what struck him most when the new day broke was how loudly and heartfelt the birds were singing in his yard. They filled the room with song through the open bedroom window upstairs. The big burr oak and maple trees in his yard now only rustled quietly.

He got up and drove down the road to survey the damage. Many of his neighbors were already out, wandering from one destroyed farm to another. Destruction and ruin were everywhere. The land was ravaged and the trees stripped bare to their white trunks. In the face of such destruction, he could only sigh a prayer. Nothing else speaks the language of the heart as eloquently.

As Brent drove into Greensburg, he was reminded of Nehemiah when he arrived in Jerusalem, and by night went out to view the walls of Jerusalem. There he found them broken down and the gates consumed with fire.

Now he saw the damage and was in awe of God's great power. A whole town was destroyed! Only a shell of a house or a building rose here and there above the rubble of hundreds of collapsed houses and buildings. It's a miracle so many survived, and not more died! Brent thought.

⋙⋘

Why were some neighbors' homes and lives left unscathed when others lost everything? It seems that, in disaster, all men are equal and common, born of the same human family. The rich, the poor, the old, the young, the sick, the healthy, the proud, the influential, all become equal when calamities strike.

Where are we safe from unforeseen destruction? Tornadoes, forest fires, earthquakes, tsunamis, floods, hurricanes, drought, volcanoes, blizzards, and dust storms — they are happening all over the world. Where in this world can you live where nature's whim cannot overpower man and make a wasteland?

Who would have ever dreamed that the beautiful ranch countryside where huge cottonwood trees dotted the green valleys, and grew to the grandeur height of eighty-five feet, would ever be changed? Just over the hill south in the Mule Creek Basin was the haunt of Brent's boyhood. And now the open highway into Greensburg that went up and over the hills, struck through a land he did not recognize.

The monster vortex that hit Greensburg was a mile and three quarter wide. One would think the tornado would just clip the town, or maybe take only half of it out as it aimlessly ambled through, inattentive to what was in its path.

After the storms passed that fateful night of May 4, Brent finally made it to bed at two o'clock. He still hadn't reached some friends, but knew most were okay.

For four nights following the storm, his candle was the only source of light as he walked about his dark farm house. He found his bed easier and earlier in these circumstances, but mysterious thoughts flooded through his mind in the reflection of the sobering time.

"Thou hast made the earth to tremble; thou hast broken it". Psalm 60:2

"Fire, and hail; snow, and vapors; stormy wind fulfilled his word". Psalm 148:8

Chapter 17

Rescue on the Way!

Ray Stegman, a storm spotter and part-time county emergency management coordinator, was watching the coming storm from three miles west of Greensburg. As he monitored the color radar display on his cell phone, he saw two hook patterns cross the county line. At 9:15 p.m. he called back to the sheriff's office in Greensburg, and told them to set off the tornado sirens. Awhile later he called again and told them to leave the sirens on.

Watching the storm from Bucklin, the Ford County Fire and EMS Chief Smith thought the wall of clouds had a strange formation, especially toward the ground. Minutes later he heard that Greensburg had suffered a direct hit. He waited a bit, to see if the first report was exaggerated. But without more information, he started driving towards Greensburg with a rescue squad (three ambulances and a fire truck.) They had to pause and wait out the strong winds and falling debris.

While Smith was coming from the west the eighteen miles from Bucklin, Pratt County emergency and medical services administrator McMannon led a rescue from the east. He waited out some high winds at Haviland. When he reached Greensburg, he drove up to a few blocks from the stop light and saw serious debris by the light of his spotlight.

McMannon set up a triage at the Dillon's Grocery Store east of Main Street and on HWY 54. It was in a good central location to have people meet and then load the ambulances going to Pratt, Dodge City and Wichita. The Greensburg hospital had been destroyed.

Stegman and Koehn, the Greensburg Fire Chief, had suffered family and personal losses in the tornado hit. They asked McMannon to take charge of the rescue. Koehn had just returned to Greensburg from a fishing trip. His family was able to talk to him on an emergency radio.

"Dad, we're all okay," they told him. "But the house is filling with gas; we can smell it." His father told them to get out as soon as possible. Koehn called Pratt, Ford and Commanche Counties, but crews came from many other counties as well.

One of the hardest things for Koehn to do was to drive on by the injured. He had to keep the overall view of helping as many as possible that night. As he drove through the damage, he thought hundreds of body bags would be needed.

McMannon turned around and requested that Koehn stick with him, as he didn't know the town. He got a telephone book out and found a map. Street signs were bent over and often gone completely. Landmarks were gone. Life-long residents of Greensburg didn't know where they were. In order to find addresses, rescue crews had to count the number of streets east or west, using Main Street as a base point. As reports of the injured came in, Koehn gave directions and McMannon relayed that to the rescue teams.

Debris on the streets was a major deterrent. At some places, an ambulance could drive in to pick up the injured, but at other times the injured had to walk or be carried. It was exhausting work.

Wichita dispatched heavy-rescue crews; and some emergency crews drove in from Oklahoma.

Because the cell tower was down, and land lines were knocked out, the rescuers used emergency radios or hand held radios for communication. There were so many anxious and injured people asking for help, and so many unaccounted for, that McMannon had to roll up his window so he could focus on the over-all picture and keep the rescue moving in an organized way.

Ambulances were everywhere in abundance. Drivers were recruited so the paramedics could help more injured.

Many farmers drove into town with equipment to clear the streets for rescue vehicles.

The first reports of death came within the hour. Two bodies were kept in a roadside bar for a while, and then a truck service building became a morgue.

Emphasis was placed on helping the living first, and marking the dead bodies with an orange cone. All over town, rescue workers were transporting the injured to Dillon's where the ambulances stood ready for service. Cars and pickups with shattered windshields and flat tires were used to transport the injured. Some of the victims stumbled in without shoes. The dispatcher at the sheriff's office gave one of them her sneakers. Others changed into the dry orange jumpsuits and sandals from the jail. The inmates from the jail were transferred as soon as possible.

The tire store started repairing tires. Some waited for up to an hour for a tire repair and then drove right back into the debris to rescue more victims.

Earl Anderson, who had had years of rescue experience, was coming from Garden City that night and noticed the police and rescue were passing him at high speeds. He thought there had been an accident ahead. When he reached the road block, they told him his town was blown away. He detoured and came into town from the north, and started on rescue efforts. He had two flats that night and has had five since. His house is gone; even the basement would not have been a safe place for him.

※

Louis Schmidt was working at the Meade hospital and noticed news of the tornado on the TV. It didn't really register with him that anything significant was going on at the time, other than a severe thunderstorm warning. As he went about his work, he suddenly took note that there was a confirmed tornado on the ground, headed straight for Greensburg.

He remembers thinking that he wouldn't be able to go on the rescue team because he was at work. However, because the need was so great, he met the Montezuma rescue team in Bucklin, and rode with them to Greensburg. They thought they might search a few houses on the outskirts of town, but that's not how it turned out. The whole town was a pile of rubble to sort through!

When their rescue team came into town, they were impressed with all the people who had shown up to help with the search and rescue effort. The air was damp and chilly, and the town was completely black except for the rescue vehicles and flashlights of the searchers. The moon peeked through the clouds occasionally and cast an eerie glow through the ghostly-looking trees.

The Montezuma team registered at the command post and waited for their assignment. When the search and rescue team was organized, they followed them in their van with an infrared camera mounted on top, slowly scanning both sides of the street with the camera. When they had proceeded three or four blocks down the street, they picked up something on the camera. One of them walked out to check it out, while the other helped direct location. They found an elderly gentleman who didn't make it out alive.

A few blocks later, they found two dogs in the back seat of a car that was almost completely covered with debris. The dogs were frantic. How did they get into that car?

They found some people who were making themselves at home in their basements and settling in for the night. Many walked around in a daze.

—◆—

At five that afternoon, Brianna Eck's alarm rang and she pressed the snooze alarm several times before she gave up sleep and headed to work at the Pratt Regional Medical Center. The hospital knew they were in a tornado watch so they were preparing the empty rooms, charting, and busily answering call lights.

Suddenly they noticed it became extremely dark outside. That's when they started to watch the weather channel. They saw there was a tornado down at Protection. Then the next thing they knew it was headed for Greensburg. One of the other nurses called her husband to see if he was okay. Brianna wasn't too worried but somehow she was talked into calling home to see if her family was in a safe place. The phone just rang and rang.

—◆—

Brianna's mother, Iris, had been listening to the weather monitor, and when they said the tornado was entering Kiowa County, her daughters Kyndra, Kara, and she debated if they should go down the cellar. All at once Iris thought of her son's wife, Jessica. She was home by herself and had no idea what was going on.

It reminded her of five years ago in May when they had to go down into the cellar because a twister was headed their way. Once again, the men weren't home until later on in the evening. That time they lost a few storm windows and a lot of trees were broke up.

Iris' husband, Howard, and son, Shannon (Jessica's husband), were getting home late after driving truck in Oklahoma. Kim was camping about 100 miles north with some friends. Iris called Jessica and urgently insisted she come to their house at once. A tornado was coming closer, and there would be hail.

Iris is a lady of action. She saw there wasn't protection for the vehicles, so they took three vehicles to Pratt. Jessica left her older car and drove Kim's car to safety from the storm. It was very windy and started to rain hard when they left, but soon they drove out of the heavy rain.

Iris took the weather monitor with her, and frequently it warned of a very large and dangerous tornado. "Seek shelter immediately!" They thought with all the lightning present, especially to the west, they would be able to see a large funnel cloud, but they couldn't see much besides a huge cloud cover.

Arriving in Pratt, they sat at the hospital parking lot, waiting, waiting. Many other cars, plus one or two school buses, also parked there.

Soon one of Kyndra's co-workers called and said several homes along HWY 183 had been taken. Then the weather monitor reported, "It looks like Greensburg will take a direct hit from the tornado."

Kyndra, still talking with her coworker when it hit Greensburg, heard that 60% of the town was hit. That was later changed to 95%.

It didn't take long for an ambulance to leave Pratt, sirens blaring and headed toward Greensburg. Ten minutes later another ambulance left, followed by several State Patrols screaming through town.

The hospital was placed into emergency mode. Extra personnel were called in; more nurses and all the doctors were needed to handle the emergencies that they were sure would come.

Meanwhile back in the hospital parking lot, Iris and the girls heard the weather monitor's incessant warning. They heard the announcement that the tornado was five miles SW of Haviland, right at Shannon and Jessica's farm location.

"It's all in God's hands," Iris told Jessica. They were so thankful they weren't at home.

Inside the hospital, Brianna finally got in touch with her trucker dad in Oklahoma. He was in his truck, and Brianna told him that the rest of the family had gone to Pratt to get out of the storm. The house supervisor came around to tell them two of Pratt County EMS's were on their way to Greensburg but were stalled because of the storm and couldn't get through.

Extra help started to show up at the hospital to get ready for injured victims. Kyndra called to tell her about the damage. The cell service was poor so all she could hear was that there were windows broken out.

While they were waiting for admissions, five beds were prepared for emergency patients. Running down to the sun room, Brianna noticed three ambulances had arrived and were waiting to unload their patients. More ambulances lined up on the street all the way to the swimming pool. One helicopter was on the ground, and two were in the air waiting to land.

The first patient arrived wrapped in a soggy, dirty blanket. When a co-worker came running around the corner calling, "Help!" Brianna ran as fast as she could to help in ICU.

The night progressed with more patients coming in from Greensburg. By night's end, they received the fourteenth patient from surgery, and the total treated that night was around eighty.

Chapter 18

"Those Are My People"

When Dr. Cannata heard the Greensburg people were being brought to Pratt by ambulance and rescue vehicles, he turned to his wife Julie and said, "Those are my people."

He left for the hospital. Julie knew she wouldn't see him the rest of the night. A kindly man, he had practiced in Greensburg, and when he moved his practice to Pratt, many of his previous patients followed him. He has been the kind of doctor everyone needs: supportive and accepting responsibility.

<hr>

After the warnings moved on about 10 miles to the northeast in the Trousdale area, Iris and the girls decided to go back to see if they still had a home. They knew traffic was not allowed past Haviland, except for emergency vehicles, so they rerouted and zigzagged through the country until they arrived home. The dairy barn had landed close to the house, a big elm had snapped off, and a cedar tree was uprooted.

Twelve windows had broken out, and the room was a shambles with all the rain, mud, and shattered glass. Cabinet doors stood open, throw rugs were tossed about and some plaster had come off the ceiling. Jessica's car had hail damage and damage from flying debris, and couldn't be moved because of so much rubble around it.

After their initial investigation, they took the four-wheel drive pickup and drove down to Shannon and Jessica's house seven miles to the southwest.

They found the house intact, but the electricity was off. It was still very windy and gusty with occasional rain.

Iris and girls went back home for the rest of the night and waited for the men to come home. The men both got as far as Haviland, but were held up because no trucks were allowed. Only emergency vehicles had access to the road for the rest of the ten miles west into Greensburg. All they could see were red and blue lights flashing on ambulances, rescue trucks, sheriff's vehicles, and state patrol cars. They were all headed west to help with the emergency.

———◆———

Kyndra Eck, RN, went to work that morning at Pratt Regional Hospital with only two hours of sleep. She debated about calling in that she couldn't come, but then she decided there were nurses who had worked all night and they needed to go home. She was better off than some of her co-workers who were still at work, even though they had lost their homes. They needed to go deal with their problems, find their families, and get some sleep.

The road to work that morning was crowded with ambulances, a National Guard convoy, and other emergency rescue vehicles. Emergency vehicles filled any other spare space. The doctor's parking lot overflowed with vehicles as well. Some of them had been at the hospital all night.

When Kyndra walked into the hospital, all the lights were on and there were people everywhere. Emergency had taken in eighty patients throughout the night. The hospital was full and had to send some patients to Wichita and to Hutchinson. She and three other nurses working on the medical floor cared for a total of twenty-three patients on that floor, most of them tornado victims.

One elderly gentleman was badly cut, bruised and muddy. He had ridden the storm out in his old trailer house in a rocking chair and was brought in by ambulance. When he arrived at the ER, the doctor cut his overalls off. That was a blow to him, because all his other clothes were gone with the tornado! The doctor came in an hour later and dismissed him.

Before the doctor left his room, he gave him a gentle touch and said, "I personally will go get you a new pair of overalls." The old man may not have believed the doctor, but about an hour later, the doctor came back with a brand new pair of overalls. The patient grinned from ear to ear.

Two pharmacies serviced the town of Pratt that night. Because some patients had no money after the storm, the pharmacies dispensed three to four days worth of free medication. Social workers collected clothes for the people who were going home.

Some of the patients who came into the hospital were fortunate to be alive, as they had refused to go down into their basements. These people were walking miracles.

Another lady, very emotional after her ordeal, told of how she had sent her children into a little crawl space in the basement. Then she took refuge under a bed. When she emerged after the storm, she was glad and amazed to find her children unharmed. Her husband had been gone, and when she told him about their close call, he reminded her that there was a loaded gun under that bed, and it was pointing straight at her as she was laying there. She felt so lucky to be alive!

As the day wore on, families tried to locate each other. American Red Cross set up a shelter for refugees in the Haviland and Mullinville gyms. The victims could come and sign in; Red Cross would then post their names on a web site, stating that they were alive and at a shelter.

The doctors came in and out all day. Some went home early and took a nap and came back later to dismiss the patients who were able to leave the hospital. Other doctors stayed around all day.

News media from as far away as New York City were everywhere you looked. They wanted to talk to victims from the tornado and everyone involved.

Kyndra went home that evening very tired. Christian Disaster Relief had been to their place and hooked up a generator. The yard was cleaned up so they could at least drive into the yard.

<hr />

Back at work on Monday, Kyndra cared for a woman who told her that after the tornado passed over their farm you couldn't even see there had been a house on the location; even the basement was gone! Her husband was killed in the tornado. She said they had gone down into the basement when they saw that the tornado was headed for their neighborhood.

They had gone to one part of the basement and settled in one corner. The noise of the storm roared around them. Her husband decided to go shut the door to the room they were in. Before he got back, the tornado hit.

A tree landed on her, trapping her, but protecting her head from the flying debris. Her husband was approximately ten feet away trapped under a pile of bricks from the outside of the house. She said that while they laid there and waited for help to arrive, she and her husband had called out to one another. It didn't take long until her husband wasn't responding any more. She knew he was gone. They had been married nearly 50 years.

Their son lived approximately a mile from their place, and he came over as soon as it was safe. The son called for an ambulance, and they got her out from under the tree. Then they began digging her husband out of the rubble of bricks, which took several hours, only to find no signs of life. The family faced planning a funeral, figuring out where their mother was going to stay, and wondering if she would be able to make it to the funeral.

The following days were filled with cleaning up the wreckage. Ten or fifteen workers at Pratt Hospital lost their homes. Some other workers helped them sort through their belongings. Others worked extra shifts for them. Everybody was willing to help out wherever they could.

It has been said the workers at Pratt Hospital are 'family.' At a time like this, that is obvious.

Dick McGowan and his friends, Darin Brunin and Derek Shaffer, were running on very little sleep. By the end of May 5, they would witness eight other tornadoes in the same area; some tornadoes overlapped each other.

Since that night, Dick still thinks about Greensburg all of the time. It has changed his perspective on storm chasing, as well as life in general. The three of them can't even begin to put themselves in the victims' shoes. It was a miracle that more people weren't killed.

There were twelve tornadoes on the evening and night of May 4. The Greensburg tornado was an EF5, growing into a 1.7 mile wide tornado and it was on the ground for twenty-two miles. Estimated damage was $153 million.

The tornado NE of Greensburg at 10:03 p.m. grew into a two-mile wide monster and was rated as a strong EF3 tornado. It was on the ground for twenty-one miles.

For three days the area suffered unstable weather and those working outside noticed the clouds more than they normally did. Tornado warnings were so frequent that people started to ignore them. The town of Greensburg was evacuated more than once because of bad weather.

One day while disaster relief workers gathered at church for a meal, a tornado was spotted on the ground to the east. With four hundred people in the building and no shelter from tornadoes close by, the warning was sounded but the meal hour continued. Someone commented, "God knows where we are."

Chapter 19

The Morning After ...

Saturday morning came slowly. It had been a long night of united prayer. Victims were scattered into the homes of family and friends, thankful for a refuge from the wind and storm.

With the light of dawn, the people of Greensburg realized they weren't any match for the workload. Houses and belongings lay in piles. There might be things to salvage if they could be retrieved before more rain drenched them.

Eric Unruh knew he had brethren to the west who could come and were just a phone call away, if only the phones were working. Fortunately, Brent Haynes from Michigan got through on the cell phone. Eric asked him to relay the information to the brethren in western Kansas. He should tell them to go south at the HWY 183 and HWY 54 junction, and there would be plenty to do.

Marlysa, Shayla, Mandi and Titus went to school to help save books there. Eric and Fern headed for town, coming in from the south. Jason and Renae went to check on Renae's clients. Numbed by what they saw, they realized they could see all the way across town! Piles and piles of debris littered the town wherever they looked. Stark, leafless trees poked their bare heads above it all. It looked like a bombed-out war zone, but no war and no enemies.

All were more aware than ever how much everyone in the community cared about each other and were cared for.

Eric walked toward Robert's house while others found Eunice standing in her desolate house on the foundation surrounded with a few parts of a wall. Looking through a large broken living room window she said, "I think this foundation will work for my new house." This was truly amazing! If Eunice could rise up from the rubble with plans for the future, others could too.

Eric returned from Robert's house, reporting that some of his children were uneasy because they still hadn't found their father. However, they had been assured that Robert and Richard had been seen walking on the street after the tornado.

Next they checked out Grandma Mae's closet where she was safely sitting until Jerry picked her up. Some books and small furniture were salvaged there.

Soon Christian Disaster Relief (CDR) crews began to arrive, which was a great comfort to the community. If you have never been there yourself, you cannot imagine the immense comfort to see brethren driving in to help when you are walking about in shock, not knowing what to do first.

Don came back from the emergency room with a badly bruised shoulder and stitches above his eye. When they finally got to bed around 3:00 a.m., sleep was hard coming.

When Don and Shana got to their house later that morning, her mother, Virginia, was already sweeping up glass in the kitchen. In the daylight it looked so much worse, but they were thankful for what they did have, and that there was no water damage.

Volunteers continued arriving to help. By the time the rains came the next day, they had the windows in Don's house boarded up, and the roof was patched.

Several days after the tornado, Shana found grass and glass in the chocolate QUIK container. The lid had been on before and was back on again. Within a week, work crews had their garage back up and the roof re-shingled. Two months later the windows were stained and varnished and ready to be put back in. What a ray of sunshine after living with boarded up holes for so long, though Shana mentioned that Don had thanked God for boarded up windows one noon meal at the table; boards to keep the bugs and wind out.

Don and Shana want to take this opportunity to say "Thank you for all the help, support, meals, and prayers that were offered on their behalf and for the congregation. We couldn't have done it without you! May God richly bless each one!"

As the night went on, Garth's house on the hill continued to collect the homeless neighbors. Lloyd and Anita, Tina and her children, Dan and Deb and their children were finally all gathered in and there they spent the night. Some slept, and some didn't. They walked around in shock, looking out windows, not believing this was for real.

During the night Anita went upstairs and found Dan at the dining room window.

"What is that light blinking at your place?" he asked. She looked out and there was a light blinking, blinking, blinking. It was an eerie sight.

"I don't know," she said. "Could someone be there? Maybe someone is checking to see if anyone is still there?" Later they found out the 4-way flashers on the pickup had been jarred on during the storm. They blinked until someone turned them off in the morning.

And what a morning it was! Before they all went their separate ways they gathered in the dining room for a special prayer of thanksgiving.

People began to show up to help. What an outpouring of love and care they felt! These people worked like beavers. There must have been about sixty people working at Lloyd's place going through the piles of debris, looking for anything worth saving. And that wasn't the only place where people cleaned, hauled, and searched. Lloyd's brother Leonard arrived from Ulysses to help where he could. Calling back to the CDR men back home, he said, "Imagine the worst you can and then multiply it by ten." The various congregations brought enough generators to set up nearly every one with power.

Anita, who had put her purse on a door knob in the sewing room before the storm, thought it was lost in the rubble. To her surprise, it was found in the van on the console between the two front seats — a little bit dirty but perfectly fine and everything in it. Lloyd said, "The Lord put it there." Anita believes it.

During the clean up they found only one completely intact wall motto. It read: "He who hath helped thee hitherto, will help thee all thy journey thru."

Among all the telephone calls Lloyd received, he especially treasures the one from his Dad and Mom. They said they were praying for them. There were two main things they wanted God to grant Lloyd and Anita. The first was that they would not become bitter; and the second, that they would remain courageous. Thank God for praying parents!

Lloyd and Garth's sixteen-foot job trailer full of tools and supplies had literally disappeared. All that was ever found of it was one axle and part of another. The skid steer was the only thing standing on the 110 ft. long floor of the shop. It looked like all the big tools had been swirled around and around and then dumped over the side. They were all ruined. Not one rafter was found. The floor of their house has never been seen. Where did it all go? They were told this tornado had a terrifically large debris cloud.

In life before the tornado, Lloyd and Anita enjoyed hearing and seeing the many songbirds in their yard. It was a great disappointment to discover they had all disappeared – not one in sight. The silence was deafening. It took a whole month for a Killdeer pair to show up. They miss the trees, too. So many birds made their home in the big pines and cedars and cottonwoods by the road. They miss the apple tree that gave them seven bushels of apples one year.

The first meal at church for all those people was a miracle in itself. It was like the feeding of the five thousand. A little from here and a little from there and there was plenty for all. A friend leaned to Anita and said, "You have a large family." She's right. And what a blessing it is; always, but especially at a time like this.

Saturday night it started raining, and did not quit until they had three inches. They felt sorry for the people in town who for safety reasons had not been allowed to return to their homes Saturday morning to retrieve what they could before it rained.

Aaron and Carmen (Lloyd's daughter from West Point, Mississippi) came to help for a few days. Carmen felt like they were coming to a funeral. In a way it was the funeral of her home, the only home she had known while growing up. Lloyd's son, Eric, and his wife, Martha, also came and helped for about a week.

As recovery went on, Anita would look over the neighborhood from Garth's house and see the fires from burning rubble. The one that bothered her the most was the fire to clean up what was left of Roger's house. Was it the finality of it all?

Lloyd and Anita lived at Garth's house for a week until the Wall family from Louisiana offered them the use of one of their RV's, which they parked on Garth's yard. The Wall's were people they didn't even know! It was such a blessing to have a little place to call home, if only the weather would have settled down. So many storms, so much wind and the RV would rock. Maybe if they hadn't weathered a tornado, it wouldn't have bothered them so much. Sometimes it seemed like they were spending half their nights in Garth and Lisa's basement.

After almost seven weeks they were finally able to move into a FEMA trailer set up on Garth's yard.

Many times, with their things scattered here and there, they have felt somewhat in pieces; a piece here and a piece there. Some of their things were stored at Garth's house, some in the container at the shop, and some in the trailer, but where? There are many frustrations.

They decided almost right away to not rebuild their house at the same place. Lloyd said he didn't want to build on a graveyard. The basement walls had some cracks from the floor being torn off. So it was dug out, filled with dirt and smoothed over. No one would ever know they had lived there for 28 wonderful years and raised four children there.

They plan on building a new house sometime next year, somewhere in the pasture. Right now the shop will come first. They are settled in a brand new FEMA trailer and very thankful to be there. The FEMA people have been very good to them, making sure everything works and that they are happy and satisfied. It is so good to live in a country that provides a house and furnishings totally free when you truly need it. And it's amazing how soon a place can start feeling like home. They are thankful for it all.

Soon after the tornado, this song kept going through Anita's mind: "Fade, Fade, each earthly joy, Jesus is mine..." It was a great comfort to her because she had to think that even though they have lost much, still 'Jesus is mine,' and nothing can take that away, not even the strongest tornado.

Lloyd and Anita are very grateful and overwhelmed by the support and care they have received from their family, friends, and all the CDR workers. Church people loaned them vehicles to drive, brought them some food and money, bought them clothes, replaced their Bibles and songbooks, prayed for them and hugged them. They say they got everything they needed and are very, very thankful!

Dan's family arrived at Rod and Lisa's by seven the next morning. After a cereal breakfast, Dan's headed for their place and Rod's took Dorothy to the old home place. They met Tim and Christine, who had driven the five and a half hours from Hiawatha. After seeing the wreckage in the daylight, they dug in and went to work. The bathroom and laundry room walls were all standing. They were able to retrieve much of the kitchen and laundry, including the washer, dryer, freezer, fridge and stove.

CDR volunteers from various places began to arrive. A young man appeared and asked if he could help. He was from Germany and was in the U.S. as an exchange student.

Sunday, May 6, was the strangest Sunday they experienced in their life. Wet and muddy belongings showed up at Rod's house, and it kept raining and storming. CDR and heavy equipment were working at Dorothy's, digging

"Smoke from burning rubble"

Marsha, Mrs. Roger Yost

huge holes to bury rubble. They made piles of brush and debris to burn, and the search for salvageable things continued. Someone found Dorothy's purse, filthy and muddy, but intact.

By this time many pickup loads of salvageable belongings were brought to available sheds in the congregation, too. Finally, when all had been recovered that could be, Dorothy granted permission to bulldoze the house down. It was so wet by now that anything they did find was in poor shape. But it was hard to see the house go. Sturdily built, the old house didn't just tumble – it took some pushing.

At lunchtime some people at church offered to help at the house. Dorothy and Lisa weren't sure if they needed help, but seeing the mess that awaited them at home, they called back and accepted the good offer. Soon five willing workers came to help. They cleaned while Dorothy and Lisa sorted ten garbage sacks of dirty, muddy, and wet laundry.

On Tuesday when they came over the last hill heading home, there was no white house, no home place to meet the eye — just dismal smoke rising. Is that what it felt like after an Indian massacre on the Kansas prairies?

Chapter 20

God Is Still Good

President Bush was coming to town, and Wednesday was to be the day! Rod and Lisa left for town later in the morning. They were hoping Lani would get to see him on her birthday. They were too late! When they tried to enter town, security would not let them in.

There was much to be done back home, though. Ladies were working on Dorothy's belongings back at Eric's shed, so they went over there. It was just so overwhelming! After lunch at church, Lisa went back with seven ladies she hadn't known before and spent all afternoon working together with them. What to keep? What was precious? What to clean? What to throw away? These were the questions they faced. They did find some treasures that could be saved, but there was much to burn, too. Meanwhile, Dorothy had a meeting with nine MUA men at her home place to survey the damage. They went home after supper, and some dear people Lisa didn't even know, dropped off clean laundry of Dorothy's and some cinnamon rolls.

Another ray of cheer: there was a man from Louisiana who offered to loan two RV's to victims. Dorothy was able to get one set up at Rod's yard the following week.

<hr/>

Sunday, Mother's Day, was the first church service following the tornado. Emotions were very near the surface as the congregation sang, "On Christ, the solid Rock, I stand, all other ground is sinking sand..." and "God moves in a mysterious way His wonders to perform. He plants His footsteps on the sea and rides upon the storm." A comforting message was brought by Minister Orville Koehn from Galva, Kansas.

Salvation Army, FEMA, Red Cross, and others set up headquarters in Haviland. They handed out vouchers for Wal-Mart, gas, and others and helped with IRS questions. AT&T came out to set up households with a new land-line and their old phone number, all at no cost.

CDR responded quickly, and there was a deep appreciation for all the volunteers who came to help from near and far. What an incredible network of volunteers! Many received sheets, comforters and towels. There was so much to be thankful for!

Tina and children were invited to live with Carl and LaVada Yost, where they stayed for more than three months. They were welcomed like family. Tina felt like she couldn't have found a better refuge. She later moved into the double-wide trailer set up on the Unruh old home place where the white house had stood.

The morning after the tornado when Terrill and Krista drove back to Roger's place, they thought they would drive into Roger's 'yard', but all they found were a few stark, bare trees left. The sheds were mere pieces of tin wrapped around what was left of the trees. Terrill's pickup was smashed. It and most of the other vehicles, looked like they had been rolled. The tractors and combine cabs were crunched. One implement was folded as if it were no more than a piece of paper. The trash strewn over the yard was incomprehensible.

Krista walked into what was left of the house. The roof was gone. Everything was full of dirt, glass, and straw. It was a hopeless situation.

Could this be the same cozy kitchen they had eaten in only the night before? Where was the beautiful pink crab-apple tree? How ruthlessly the garden and flowerbeds had been destroyed! It appeared that no one cared about this place... but oh! how their hearts ached as they remembered the good times...

The week before, the family had enjoyed dinner and the afternoon together. The weather was beautifully pleasant and sunny. Most of the cousins had eaten lunch on the porch. In the afternoon, they had walked around the yard, admiring the flowers and the garden that was already up in neat, straight rows. They had walked out to Tara's flower garden, somewhat secluded by the trees and talked while they perched on the logs and rocks. Some were seated on the wooden swing or had pulled chairs up on the patio bricks that Terrill had laid when he was still at home. Others had relaxed on the lawn, and the children had swung in the hammock. The shade trees protected them from the sun's brilliant rays.

Now it was gone, demolished in a few minutes!

Two weeks after the tornado:

Terrill and Krista felt a need of rejuvenation so they packed a lunch and headed for Triple Ponds. A brisk spring breeze was blowing, but they didn't care. The grass was green, the trees were still standing, and the ponds held a nice amount of water. They sat on the deck of a cabin and enjoyed the sandwiches, chips, potato salad, carrots and grapes.

After a time of relaxation, they started on a short hike across the pasture and over a bluff to another small pond. The hills in the distance were a picturesque sight with numerous trees adorning them. The white yuccas gave character to the setting, and wildflowers bloomed abundantly. Little white daisies with their intricate petals and yellow button centers bloomed along with bright yellow flowers, orange ones and purplish-blue ones with a dozen or so draping on one stem. A bright pink cactus flower hidden among the taller grass suddenly caught their eyes, making them catch their breath. It seemed to say, "Life may give you prickles, but there is still beauty to behold!"

The seeping ground told them there was a spring nearby. A school of minnows swam past as they jumped across the creek. Soon they came to the little spring-fed pond. Bright blue damsel-flies and black and white dragonflies darted closely above the water. They climbed a grassy bluff where they sat down to breathe deeply of the scene before them. Turtles bobbed in and out of the water. Two birds chirping to each other across the pond, and the frogs croaking in the background, made a peculiar trio. They decided that they had found the prettiest spot in their home state of Kansas.

As they took it all in, they were reminded that God's world is still beautiful, and He is still good.

"For here we have no continuing city, but we seek one to come. By him therefore let us offer the sacrifice of praise to God continually...giving thanks to His name." Hebrews 13:14-15

Chapter 21

Added Burdens Bring More Grace

Joe and Karen Yost's home was still standing, and it was such a nice, dry shelter that night for the grandparents and Aaron's. It looked so good after seeing the devastation in town. But time soon showed the damage done to their house, too. The siding was damaged, and windows were broken out. Doors would not shut properly, making one wonder if the house has shifted in the storm. The oil shed needed a new west wall where the stack of oil barrels had flown around, gouging anything they hit. The shed needed a new paint job and new doors, and there was considerable damage to the trees.

As an MUA man, Joe was busy with damage assessment and bookwork for many days. The executive board offered to come in and help with the administration and lift his load.

———◆◆◆———

Bryce and Diane woke up to a new world outside their home on May 5. Diane tried to help Bryce salvage tools and parts from what had been his paint shop. The south wall was standing due to a tractor and baler that remained anchored there during the storm. And the garden? Shards of glass and wood were strewn about, along with twisted fence and mangled plants. Bryce's large storage cabinet containing paint supplies had landed on one end... so much for the feeling of satisfaction the night before.

Diane received many phone calls from her family over the next days, and she just couldn't keep back the tears. What a comfort to be with other sisters during this time.

Bryce and Diane were part of the Dodge City Mission Outreach, and on Saturday, some of these dear friends arrived. Bryce and Diane felt that they were the least of anyone who needed help. They wished they could go to Roger and Marsha to help out there, but now the crews were moving onto their yard, too. They stood back in amazement as one vehicle after another drove into the yard, and CDR crews went to work. Chainsaws buzzed, skid steers zipped back and forth moving branches, and the old barn was pushed in a heap. It continued to rain, turning the once green lawn into a sodden, muddy mess.

One older gentleman kindly took the time to try to encourage Diane. "There surely will be more grace during this time," he said. That will always be a special memory for her.

Bryce rushed about trying to organize all the volunteers. You wouldn't have guessed he'd just had surgery.

One day as they stepped into church for another delicious, hot meal, someone stopped Diane to tell her someone was coming over to rake her yard. The work had seemed so overwhelming to her, knowing that their baby was due in a couple of weeks. It was so enjoyable working with so many friends. Her goal has been: "As ye have therefore received, freely give."

God answered many prayers during this time. Bryce has recovered from the surgery very well, and their little son, Andrew, arrived healthy and not only on time, but a day early!

Life is fairly normal again. Green has returned where once it was mud, the garden is bearing bountifully, and an added blessing is the FEMA trailer on the yard — not just the trailer itself, but what it houses inside — loved ones safe from the storm.

＊＊＊

Ryan and Roger caught a ride with the storm chaser who was going by to see what happened on Ryan's yard. The house was somewhat damaged but still standing. They found Ryan's pickup still drivable, so they now had one vehicle.

Later that night when Ryan and Rachelle stopped by their house to pick up a few necessities, they felt a mixture of guilt and relief. Their house was still standing. It would've been so much easier for them to start over, rather than someone who had put years of work into their place.

"But God sees all things," RaChelle says. "We've all agreed that, although we were terrified of the storm, there was calm in our hearts. God was there through it all. We cannot thank Him enough for protecting us. The results of the storm will be long-lasting, but we trust there will be a way."

———————

Friday night was a sleepless night for Roger and Marsha. When morning finally came, they decided to go to what used to be their place.. Marsha was in the same dirty dress and big mud boots she had worn to mulch her garden the day before.

How could they ever be prepared for the devastation that daylight revealed? The destruction can hardly be described. Broken and uprooted trees, fields and pastures strewn with debris, and dead and wounded cattle were grim evidence of the tornado's path. Very little was recognizable of the farm site. The round top sheds were reduced to sheets of twisted metal hanging from what remained of the trees. The roof of the house was gone and the siding was no longer white, but a dirty brown color. Roger's bedroom on the south end of the house was totally gone.

The wrecked vehicles gave evidence, however, that this was indeed their place. The pickups, farm trucks, and machinery, together with Ryan's car, Terrill and Kristas' two vehicles, and the car Chadd had recently purchased, were hardly recognizable. They were too shocked to even cry. A huge oil battery tank from a half-mile north had been flung onto the house by the whirling tornado, landing on the supporting wall next to where they were huddled.

Shock brought Roger and Marsha through the first few days following the tornado. How can one's mind grasp so much? In just a few minutes they had become homeless. They appreciated so much the tremendous amount of support and help from both the home congregation and surrounding congregations. People came prepared to work, and most of all, to support them in their disaster.

The main feeling the first few days, following the tornado, was still one of thankfulness that they had all survived. Marsha wishes she could say that negative feelings have never come since then, but that would not be true. There has been a roller coaster of emotions including denial, anger, sadness, frustration, depression and near despair. But mingled together with the negative feelings have been thankfulness, courage, and hope. Life goes on, and they are beginning to learn how to live again.

Some of the simple things we take for granted can be cause for frustration in the days following the tornado. "Where is a nail clipper? I'm sure I saw one somewhere." No one knows. It seems to take twice as long to do anything. But the very hardest thing for Marsha has been a sense of not belonging anywhere. There is no evidence of what they once called "home". When deprived of it, it is a loss keenly felt. Home is the best place to be after a long, stressful day. It's your little corner of the earth where you "belong." Marsha was keenly aware of the fact that, anywhere they went, they would be disrupting someone else's life. It was almost like they were now 'in the way' here on earth.

Financial strain and many decisions to face when you're already overwhelmed added to their load. Most people can tolerate some loss in life, but what if almost everything is taken? Coverage on an older house doesn't go very far when you think of rebuilding. Is rebuilding the wise thing to do? If not, where should they go, and what should they do? About the third or fourth day after the storm, the house was pushed in and burned. Marsha remembers receiving an almost eerie feeling driving back to her parent's yard around dusk after supper at the church. The fires smoldering at their place and the neighbors' places finalized a part of their lives that was gone.

They lived in a little camper trailer for three weeks, but the feeling of already being overwhelmed, together with being very crowded and always looking for things, made them all a little edgy. One particularly difficult morning, (Chadd wasn't able to be there), but Roger, Tara and Marsha were all crying during devotions. Roger read from Isaiah 40, verses 28-31, reminding them again that the Lord would renew their strength if they would wait upon Him.

They moved into a FEMA home set up on Bryce's yard. Roger had been acquainted with FEMA while working on the Christian Public Service board for the last ten years. It is a new twist to now be living in one of their homes!

They have planned a house, which is presently under construction in central Kansas. At first they were hardly capable of planning a new home. Most anything would have sounded good – they just needed a home.

And there were the fears that came after the tornado, a very real part of their life. In the past Marsha had enjoyed thunderstorms, but that all changed. The possibility of a storm moving in almost made her feel panicky. She could hardly relax enough to sleep at night, and then in the morning, she did not want to get up to face the day. They spent several nights in her parent's basement rather than brave it out in the little camper trailer.

Roger and Marsha's lives will never be the same again, and it reminds them of a much bigger change that is coming that will make this one seem so insignificant. We could well be going about our everyday life, thinking it's a normal day when the great Judgment Day comes. Where will our FINAL home be? May it be a glorious one for each of us!

Saturday morning after Dan and Deb left Garth's house, they stopped at Rod and Lisa's. It is amazing how traumatized you can be and still talk normally. They drove past the piles of debris on Lloyd and Anita's and Tina's places, past the damaged school and the demolished teacher's house. Bryce's paint shop and barn were gone. Beyond Dorothy's place and just past the corner they met a small herd of cattle meandering down the road. They were Dan's heifers from the pasture east of their house. It was a miracle. Herding them east down the gravel road, they put them in a pasture. Thankfully, the cattle were uninjured.

The cows and calves at the school pasture didn't fare as well. Five cows and sixteen calves were lost. It was a pitiful sight. By the time, Dan and Deb reached their place, Deb's parents, Herman and Jewel, and also a neighbor, Bobby Ahrens, had arrived and they started working trying to salvage anything they could.

Gregg and Lori did not sleep well that night, even though they felt welcome at his brother, Sheldon's house.

By the next morning, they were anxious to see the damage their house had suffered. Stepping over power lines to get to the house they saw it was still standing but not a pretty sight. CDR was on the job already, cleaning up and putting plastic and tarps on the roof. What a nice gesture, Gregg and Lori thought as they surveyed their beat-up house, standing there without the barn and shed. The back screen door had blown away; the back door had blown open allowing the wind to catch the basement door and send it down the steps. The little girls found their room strewn with dirt and glass. Wind and rain came in the kitchen making a mess there. They would be able to live in the house temporarily but how would they replace it? The roof had lifted up and come back down making it structurally unsound.

By Saturday noon they had electricity and about fifteen ladies showed up to help clean. It was a great lift to have that done. They were so grateful for all the help they received; and thankful for what God had done for them.

The guests at Gordon and Betty Unruh's house rose in the morning with the invitation to stay as long as they wished. Curt and Joann enjoyed the ten or eleven days they spent with Gordon and his wife, Betty, and also the other guests, Jerry and Starla McLain, and Mae Unruh.

A friend of Curtis Unruh wrote a letter, encouraging him that there would be some good come out of this — he should wait and see. It didn't take long to see how it has brought out the good side of all his friends and neighbors. Psalm 121 has become more meaningful: The Lord is a keeper; He is a help. He watched over us, but we need to look up to the Lord more often.

Harlin's house in the town of Greensburg was beyond salvaging, but they were able to save some contents. Karla and Angie, their daughters from Michigan, were able to come help with the clean-up, and also help move them into Home Again in Haviland for a month. By then they were offered a house near town, and they were glad to have a chance to buy it.

When Aaron and Marsha were able to return to their home Monday morning, they were surprised at the devastation. The siding was ripped off, windows were blown out, and the blinds were hanging in tatters. Glass and dirt were everywhere; broken lamps, mottos and clocks littered the floor. Boards were blown in and papers were strewn about. Their garage lay scattered in pieces over their back lawn. Not one piece was standing! But they felt so fortunate, because they were able to save almost all of their things; some of it will never be quite the same again, but that's okay. They mostly felt so thankful that they escaped without any bodily harm and all their friends were also alive and well.

Aaron and Marsha and William rented a house in Wilmore. Being book agent for the church, they have spent much time doing a thorough job of getting basic books back into the homes that had suffered loss.

Saturday morning Lyndon and Denise, Elaine and Jewel, (Lyndon's mother and sister) and other friends returned to their house. As they were sifting through their precious belongings, they were told to leave town. They were able to salvage their dresser and chest of drawers, Bibles, quite a few wedding gifts and some of their dishes. They were not allowed back in until Monday morning.

The next Saturday while Lyndon and Denise were cleaning up at the house, Denise was cut badly on her leg. Lyndon took her to a mobile clinic. It was repaired with eight stitches, a tetanus shot, and antibiotics.

CDR moved in and hauled their house to the landfill that day. It felt good to have a closure, though they had enjoyed living in that cozy house.

Eunice and her son, Kent, went to town the next morning with a trailer and got a load of furniture. When they went back for a second load, they were turned back. People were kept out of town for two days while searches were conducted with search dogs. During that time, it rained several inches which lessened the chances of saving anything. Besides some of the furniture, Eunice was able to save some things from the kitchen.

Some of Grandma Mae's dresses were hanging in the rafters. Her sister Juanita had a canister set on her counter in the kitchen. After the tornado one of them had a large chunk of insulation in it. The lid was set back on!

Through it all, Grandma Mae says she never felt bitter. She just felt like God was talking and especially talking to her. Last Sunday when she left church, such a warm feeling came over her. She had been thankful, but not thankful enough to the Lord for keeping her through the storm.

About one month after the tornado, all three of Grandma Mae's children were home. Ross and Lisa Unruh live on the old home place, and they invited the family for Sunday dinner. It was very special to be 'back home.'

Grandma Mae has moved to Home Again in Haviland, and truly feels like she is 'home again!' She is happy there and thankful that she has such a nice place to live.

Daylight revealed more damage at the Howard Eck residence. Large limbs had fallen on the machinery. Grain bins were damaged as well as out buildings; many, many trees were uprooted. Fences were gone, and cattle were roaming. Iris' garden put up with a lot of Mother Nature's fury this year – floods, winds, tornado; and now cattle...

The next morning they noticed the historic granary across the road to the west had undergone drastic changes. Nearly two miles to the north, their neighbor's farmstead was demolished. A half-mile east another farmstead had suffered the same fate. Following the path of the tornado a half mile to the northeast, another farmstead and a half mile of trees lay in utter chaos. Two houses and an old barn were torn into splinters. The tornado demolished hundreds of irrigation circle systems to the northeast of them.

They were more fortunate than some others. One tower of their sprinkler system was displaced, so all they had to do was pull it straight with a tractor.

The volunteer brigade arrived on Saturday. Equipped with chain saws and four-wheelers, tree limbs were soon laid in piles and windows were boarded up. Rewiring recovered electricity, and with the tractor humming and the generator in place, water began running in the sinks. Cleanup in the house began in earnest. Several days later another volunteer came with a large loader to load the piles and haul them away.

Meals were being served at the church so Howard's family decided to attend on Saturday evening. Once again they took the weather monitor along (a person gets the jitters very quickly when one hears and sees the massive destruction that can be done by wind, hail and rain.) This time the news was "tornado spotted southwest of Haviland, take cover immediately." So instead of going west to church, they went east to Pratt for supper.

Driving through Greensburg on Sunday, they were amazed how 'lost' you can get in your own small town. Landmarks were gone. Brick buildings on Main Street lay in piles of rubble. All the street signs were gone or bent over. Greensburg will take a long time to recover and rebuild; it will never be the same again.

Chapter 22

"Open Your Mouth!"

There are stories that will be told over and over as folks remember the old Greensburg before the tornado:

A dear Grandma said she wouldn't go into a storm shelter even if the sirens were sounding. The cellars seemed too tight with so many people in them, and they weren't very comfortable. Sure enough, she rode out the storm in her tub. When the tornado blew over, she still felt safer in the tub, so that is where she spent the long night.

———◆———

Another family was out in the weather by the time it was over, too. Having no basement, they wrapped their arms and legs around a pipe. They claim the wind came through twice and they hung on both times. The house blew away with the first wind, so the second time around they were out in the hail, wind, and rain, but they managed to hang on.

———◆———

Colleen Panzer, like many of the older people, found it challenging to go down to the safety of a storm shelter or a basement. Despite her family's pleas, she did not get to safety and was severely injured in the storm. Kenny Brown heard her cries and went to her side. He found himself unable to speak. She was still talking at the time, but he still couldn't speak and didn't know why. When the EMT's came on the scene, he still wasn't speaking. One of them said: "Open your mouth." He did, and it was full of insulation.

Unfortunately, Colleen didn't survive her injuries. She had been badly hit on the head and had two broken legs with severe lacerations. A tourniquet was used on each leg and they were going to transfer her by helicopter to a larger center for treatment, but she passed away just after they became airborne.

Opal was born and raised in Kansas and completed her first eight grades at a country school in Stafford County. She rode Buttons, her horse, the two-and-a-half miles to school. The black lunch bucket opened from the top and usually had ham or peanut butter and jelly sandwiches in it. Their horse wasn't used to any double riders and on her first day of school, Opal was put on behind her brother Glen. As Glen tells the story, "I wasn't bucked off. I was pulled off by little sister!" Later she went to high school in St. John and graduated.

She looks back with regret at the sacrifice her parents made to send her to nursing school in Halstead. She didn't even complete the first year. Opal was in love. She married Lawson Freeman in 1935, at the age of 21 years. Lawson was named after Dr. Lawson and went by the nickname of 'Doc'. He owned Freeman's Produce and Feed, where they bought eggs and cream from farmers. Opal was often washing cream cans and writing out checks at 12:30 p.m. Saturday evenings so the farmers could buy their groceries.

Lawson could cull chickens better than anyone around. He could go through the farmer's flock and know which chickens would lay and those that wouldn't. Doc built Opal a new house in 1941.

Doc joined the Navy during the war. He had just finished his basic training and come home for the weekend. He doted on his little thirteen-month-old son. Doc had a riding horse at Opal's parent's farm. He was riding with Opal's brother in the pasture when his horse stepped in a hole and flip flopped, taking a bad tumble. It broke Doc's neck, and when he got to Great Bend hospital, the doctor said he was gone. Opal was still running the Produce and Feed Store. She had a chance to sell it and then she could stay home with her little son.

When her son was six years old, Opal married Walter Askins. Walter had just been released from the Air Force. Walter was a meat cutter by trade, but when his father passed away, Walt started farming in Hamilton County. The family lived in a shack out there for the summer while Walt was farming. When school started, Opal came back to Greensburg and stayed home with Jerry.

Walt had just retired from farming in 1990, when he came home from the doctor's office and told Opal the doctor had found a spot on his lung. He lived five or six years after that, enjoying working part time for Doug Harrell. He also used the garage to re-finish furniture.

Opal has lived by herself for many years. On May 4, 2007, she was sitting quietly in her living room with her big, beautiful cat, Babe. Opal noticed the hail storm outside although she was very hard of hearing and couldn't hear the sirens. She took her cat and went downstairs. When the hail let up, she came back up.

A perky 98-year-old now, she leaned forward in her blue rocking chair in a pleasant room where she now resides in Haviland. Spreading out her arms as to embrace this faithful chair, she declares, "I came back up and was sitting in this same rocker when the tornado hit."

Opal watched the family room wall come crashing in and the curtains started to blow around after the windows broke. She didn't know what to do, but God took care of her. And then a young man, a neighbor of hers, came. Through a broken window, he asked her if the door was locked, and she got up and unlocked it. He helped her out of the house, warning her, "Don't step on the glass."

Opal sat in the neighbor's yard with his wife a long time until someone came and picked her up and took her to the Dillon's parking lot. A doctor was standing there when she arrived. He inspected her, and seeing all the blood on her hand, took a look at her little finger and told her she would have to go to Pratt for surgery. She was put into an ambulance with quite a few others. When she arrived at the hospital, they took her right up to surgery.

After being discharged from the hospital, she was taken to the Haviland gym and given an army cot for the rest of the night.

Her son, Jerry, moved back from California into the basement of the damaged house and 'camped' without electricity for several months while he worked at restoring the house.

<hr>

A gentleman of Greensburg got to thinking about tornadoes a while back and went out to his shed in the back yard. He dug himself a hole in the dirt floor of his shed, closing it with a piece of plywood with a strap attached to it. Now he had a plan for himself and his wife. Should a tornado come, they would crawl into the hole and anchor the plywood. His plan worked until the plywood was sucked off and blew away. But the sky delivered a boat, which did the job nicely until it was all over. The story has it that the can with his $30,000 was safe in the shed, too.

⊰•⊱

Another man wasn't so lucky. He and his wife were in the basement and had weathered the first half of the storm, though the house and even the floor were gone. He lost his life when the storm put a pickup right down on them. His wife no longer has a husband, and they didn't have any insurance. Later it was learned how bravely she has volunteered at the Salvation Army store in Pratt, comforting others.

⊰•⊱

Little Xavier is a boy of action. His grandpa, watching the little boy, chuckles, "Yes, tornadoes come, and most of them go..."

They did not have a basement, and Xavier was already sleeping that evening, so his Dad, Bruce Raber, carried him into a closet for shelter. His cousin Haley was there, too, and he slept soundly until their ears started popping. The house was badly damaged, but repaired as soon as possible.

His mother, Lorraine, was in California at a wedding rehearsal. When they heard the tornado was hitting Greensburg, the wedding party paused while they prayed for those in its path.

⊰•⊱

Scott Huck, a crop sprayer, was spraying in the northern part of Kiowa County when he had a call from his friend that there was a tornado headed toward Greensburg, and he shouldn't come back in. He was in a tall rig and wasn't interested in riding out a storm up there in the open, so he hurried back to town and drove under the canopy at the station. The tornado took him for a ride across Main Street and placed him up against the furniture building on the other side. He had his air-conditioner going, which may have kept enough pressure in the cab to keep the windows intact.

He saw many things. When a brick went into the engine block and killed his motor, his air-conditioner quit, and the windows broke out. Before he could get out of the sprayer, he had to pull a board out of his back. He went down the street, helping others until someone spotted his injuries and sent him on priority medical need to Pratt.

———⚬———

Another story, not personally verified, is that a son in Great Bend had plans to go the next morning to see if his dad in Greensburg had suffered any damage. He walked outside, saw a paper lying in the yard and picked it up. It was the deed and title to his dad's place in Greensburg!

And harder to believe — it was heard that a mailbox from Greensburg had been found in South Dakota, with mail still intact... (PLEASE verify if this is true!)

And HARDEST to believe, with all the talk of re-building the town, and its exciting plans for beauty and being environmentally friendly — they have now decided to move the Big Well! Greenburg hasn't lost its humor, though there isn't much laughter around yet!

———⚬———

Some things are taken for granted. We think nothing will change them, but we are mistaken. Gone is:

- Hunter's Drug with the old soda fountain is gone. Faithful Dickie stirred the soda mixture, tapped the edge of the glass, and peered benevolently over his glasses at former students. He still called each one of them by name.
- The old church, housing Fran's Antiques where one could while away an hour or two in history — alone, or with someone from the age who appreciates the many unique tools, dishes, and antique furniture.
- Big Well Park where the children walked the wall after a round or two on the playground, while their parents huddled over a picnic in the shelter to get out of the Kansas wind.
- The library with Maxine and Debbie so willing to search for that favorite author, or to recommend another good old book. Those shelves harbored a wealth of old books that will be hard to replace.
- The conveniences are gone, too. The grocery store, the barber shop, the shops on Main Street, the restaurants; so many businesses have disappeared.

- Many friends are scattered and will contact ever be made? So many times questions are asked: "Where is this or that one? Are they in the surrounding towns: Dodge City, Pratt, Kinsley, Hutchinson, Bucklin, Haviland, Coldwater, and Mullinville; or gone to family further away? Are they coming back? Will a town stripped of its trees, houses, and businesses be able to pull them back?

Chapter 23

Clean-up and Re-building

Daylight didn't soften the damage to the farms down HWY 183. As many CDR crews moved in to begin clean-up and rebuilding the destroyed farms, they were told dinner would be served at the Church. That was a faith announcement. What dinner? We arrived at church and found friends from other congregations already arriving, and Susan and Sherri were already at work. They had rounded up twenty pounds of hamburger, fifteen pounds of shredded cheese, and five large bags of tortilla chips for haystacks.

We soon found the generator couldn't service the lights in the fellowship hall, the microwave, and the stoves, all at the same time. So, we settled down to frying our frozen meat as well as we could. Someone stirred up a double batch of unbaked cookies and one pan of cheerio squares. Fortunately, we didn't know we were cooking for three hundred people, or we would have panicked. Around 12:30 we put lunch on. It seemed such a puny amount of dessert, but we said lunch was ready. The ladies from western Kansas had sent packed lunches or the ingredients for preparing sandwiches. We announced that the men should all eat what we'd prepared, and then we'd use the packed sandwiches for supper.

But, the men just kept coming, and coming! When the food looked like it wouldn't feed that many people, someone brought more frozen hamburger. Then some ladies brought in a big food chest of hot burritos. These burritos were actually for their youth and parent's picnic, but served so well in this situation. Then more hamburger, fried up and seasoned, was brought in and was added to the rest. Later we laughed together when Saundra told us it was for sloppy joes!

A group of youth from Protection came in with their pastor's wife and presented us with their baked goods. They had planned on a bake sale, but decided to give their lovely baked things to us. How thoughtful of them! That was the dessert we were lacking, and was very much appreciated. (It sure stretched that double batch of unbaked cookies and cheerio squares for three hundred people!) Pans of bars mysteriously appeared, perhaps sent along with the sandwich lunches. We were overcome at the generosity of all the caring strangers who reached out to us. It reminded us of the five loaves and two fishes. We supplied an insufficient amount of food, and the Lord sent the rest.

Were we organized? No! Someone called and said they were coming. What did we need? We told them we needed supplies to make more sandwiches for a hundred and fifty people.

For that Saturday evening, a surprise 25th anniversary picnic had been planned. Now instead, the couple drove up to the church and began to unload an impressive amount of food. How did they manage to get this amount of food together on such short notice? (Several weeks later that couple found out they had delivered the lunch intended for their own 25th celebration!) We fed 250 people that evening.

It didn't stop there. The next afternoon a truck pulled in at the school with a load of lumber and supplies for the teacher's house and school. It didn't take long and a rafter was produced for a pattern. The big room of the school had a wall leaning, and because it was raining outside, they decided to make the rafters in that room. By the time the ladies took supper down there, the rafters were completed so they could set up tables to eat in there. Before they left that night, the teachers' house was waterproof, and the windows of the school boarded up.

Sunday was not a day of rest this time. We were in a disaster, and it was a work day. Other congregations also forfeited their services and came over to help. We had 535 people for dinner that day. From there on, our neighboring congregations brought in two meals a day all week.

On Saturday, a large crew of youth came to clean up rubble, walking through fields as they searched and picked up debris. Two congregations brought food for each meal that day, serving 850 at noon and 640 at supper. Sometimes they would still be serving one and a half hours later as the workers trickled in. The menus were wonderful: ham, potatoes, taco salad, grilled hamburgers, grilled chicken, chicken and rice, enchiladas, chalupa, brisket, BBQ pork sandwiches, sloppy joes, disco and sandwiches. The next week the food committee used leftovers and served meals to the crews.

A few weeks later the youth came and walked the fields again. Two congregations brought in the noon meal and served nearly three hundred.

The faithful workers fed everyone: the homeless, the workers, people from town who also lost their homes, the volunteers from near and far. We shared stories, tears, and food. We were so thankful to have enough to include our community in these meals.

One lady from another congregation sent word that she was going to Sam's. What did we need? She was given a grocery list, and she loaded her cart with far more than had been asked for. After nearly bumping into a man, she apologized and explained why her cart was so full. She noticed that the man kind of hung around near her after that. When she went to check out, he stepped up and insisted on paying for the whole bill!

One day a parade of men came through carrying boxes to the storage room. They were delivering 250 pounds of large baking potatoes from someone in Meade. Unfortunately, we will never be able to thank all the people who helped. We don't even know who they are!

A Special Thank You!

We wish we could convey to you how thankful all the victims and the rest of those involved were to have a place to come for a hot meal where they could sit down, away from the dirt and destruction of town and their destroyed farmsteads, and fellowship with friends. It was truly appreciated. May God richly bless you for all your efforts!

When congregations brought in meals, the kitchen was clean when they left and so were the floors. The fellowship hall was vacuumed and so were the entrances.

Many ladies walked in our doors, and we didn't even ask them their names. They were our sisters, and they put up with our lack of formalities. Maybe they could see how shocked and overwhelmed we all were. We look back now and wish we could personally acknowledge so many of the acts of kindness, the hugs, the whispers of prayer support, and plain hard work that proved the caring more than anything else could have. There is no way we could have possibly fed the people that week on our own. We were too overwhelmed by the magnitude of the disaster, too busy, too tired, too far from groceries...our needs were many, and you provided for them.

Chapter 24

President Bush!

The news was out! President Bush was to be in town as an encouragement to the victims of the horrific Greensburg tornado. There were excited rumors that he might even eat the noon meal at the church. Helicopters were flying over the day before, and the possibilities were there. Well, he didn't come to lunch, but quite a few in the community did get to visit with him and shake his hand.

He declared the area a disaster, and FEMA moved in with a great deal of support and help. Around 350 FEMA trailers were set up in a special trailer court southwest of town. These were clean, new trailer houses, with up to three bedrooms, equipped with basic dishes, furniture, beds, and towels.

FEMA workers were putting in long days and dealing with frustrated people. One day a simple act was observed that showed the care that was still shining through. A FEMA worker was seen bending over to pick something up. A little later she was observed half crawling under a parked vehicle to get another 'something'. When asked what she was doing, she replied, "These people have suffered enough. They don't need a flat tire today. We have come to relieve the suffering, and we often wonder how we can do that." She was gathering nails off the street on her way to work.

Mike Umscheid of the National Weather Service Dodge City, Kansas, recalls the following Wednesday as being another wild day for him, and hopefully the last one for awhile! The evening prior, he received a phone call from U.S. Senator Pat Roberts of KS expressing his congratulations on a job well done by him and his colleagues at the office on that fateful evening. He was invited to take part in the Presidential visit to Greensburg. He was on a short list of individuals to be present in a closed door briefing at the makeshift operations control center just outside the courthouse in Greensburg.

Mike left for Greensburg about 8:30 a.m. About halfway there, he received a phone call from Air Force One. (He thinks Senator Roberts passed along his cell phone number.) It was The President! He offered his congratulations on a job well done to him and the office on getting the warnings out in a very timely and efficient manner. It was definitely an honor he will never forget!

They arrived in Greensburg after waiting in a fairly long line along HWY 54 and met with the Director of the National Weather Service who was there with the Central Region Director of the National Weather Service.

After standing in the rain for awhile, Mike had to get ready to go into the meeting room where the President was going to conduct a briefing. The President entered the room after an hour, and they all introduced themselves and shook the President's hand. Once again, the President offered his congratulations on a job well done. Towards the end of the briefing, the FEMA Director wanted to make a special acknowledgment to him and the staff at NWS-DDC for their performance. Mike spoke briefly before the group, acknowledging that it was really a well-coordinated effort by the six people working in their office that evening that made the flow of information in and out of the office so efficient.

After the formalities were over, Mike met with Larry and Scott from NWS-DDC and toured the damage so they could see it for themselves. What really impressed them the most was all the damage to brick buildings. Many of the brick buildings along Main Street were three or four bricks thick with no real "point of entry" for the wind. The High School destruction was also unbelievable, an extremely well-built structure from 1937, which had been no match for this tornado.

———⊰⋅⊱———

Generators were donated by other congregations. Volunteer electricians hooked them up. Gas was provided on the church yard, and everyone had lights when they went home at the end of the day. What a comfort that was.

Congregations donated Bibles, fabric, books, songbooks, towels, tea towels, mottos and beautiful bowls, all of which planted a hope for a better tomorrow.

One congregation offered to adopt one of our homeless young couples. We took them into a corner of the sanctuary of our very busy church. The wife put her hands over her face and cried tears of joy while we told them about the offer. They felt like there were so many people caring so much.

A week after the disaster, all of our homeless were in need of that kind of attention. Of fifty-four households in the Greensburg congregation, there were seventeen houses destroyed, thirteen houses badly damaged, and twenty-four houses undamaged, though some of those had other damage such as vehicles, fences or downed irrigations systems.

The need for personal caring and encouragement was even greater than monetary help. Arrangements were made for two congregations to 'adopt' one of these hurting families and just care for them and their needs. These victims were very appreciative of the many caring efforts of their adopted congregations. We still hear expressions of how comforting it was to have someone reach out to them.

Sometimes ladies called up and asked if they could help with anything besides meals. We admitted there was an endless amount of work, and they started pouring through the church doors, too, ready to help. They were dispatched to sheds where piles of filthy miscellaneous items needed to be sorted, scrubbed, packed, and labeled — hours and hours of dirty work. At the end of the day they would insist on taking the big black trash sacks full of nearly unsalvageable clothes and bedding to wash. Some loads took three or four washings to get them clean. They came back neatly washed, folded, delivered and labeled with little notes of encouragement and love.

Did love notes ever sing a sweeter song than that of cheerful service? Those ladies were talked about for weeks. One group of ladies worked their way through the piles of dirty things, and when they came to the end of that, they walked into homes that had opened their doors to some of the homeless. They dusted and cleaned. Then they went out to the yard and washed the vehicles. Washing a vehicle isn't glamorous CDR work, but what a lot of caring it showed!

One morning some ladies burst in the church door... ambitious, cheerful, and somehow they felt like a fresh breeze. They worked their way through piles of dirty furniture, dishes and whatever needed cleaning. Halfway through the afternoon they came in again, willing to start a new project with as much gusto as the first one. What an inspiration they were to us!

Yet another group of ladies came with such good cheer and fun in their eyes. To hear their happy banter reminded us of happier days we once knew. We were fascinated with them...swinging their rags and teasing each other about getting dirty. Would we ever laugh like that again?

Congregations brought us milk, eggs, cinnamon rolls, coffee cake and fruit; and had a fridge stocked for all of us. They brought us generators the first day and continued to supply gas for them right there on the church yard. We were taken care of in so many ways by people we didn't know, but they were our brethren. Upstairs, the church became a mini department store with toothbrushes, toothpaste, Tylenol PM, clothes, TP, and canned goods. They brought clothes and shoes, and then new bedding, towels, and comforters started coming in. Our homeless had their needs filled, and then the churches' sewing circles started to accommodate our friends. What a joy it was to pass on some of their handiwork to our 'homeless' friends, too.

Chapter 25

CDR Work Continues

Christian Disaster Relief was there to supply help after the tornado, and they brought their ambitious wives with them. They spiffed up the restrooms and filled paper towel containers and refilled soap containers.

On Friday, May 11, after the search and rescue work was ended, CDR decided that it was time to find out what could be done to help the residents of the town get their lives back to normal. By this time, the residents had a little time to themselves to sift through the piles of debris, looking for anything worth saving.

Midmorning found CDR at the central command post which actually covered a number of city blocks surrounding the damaged but serviceable courthouse. Huge RV's and semi trailers from a whole cross section of the government including the EPA, FEMA, National Guard, and numerous nearby local governments were parked there. There was even a complete mobile hospital on site.

CDR's first contact was with the Greensburg emergency manager who needed a damaged house moved off its foundation. CDR assured him that they could help him clear it off within the week. The city clerk in the new mobile office was contacted next, and she promptly handed over a list of names of city employees whose houses were ready to be bulldozed. Most of the employees had been so busy, that they had not even had time to go through their own belongings for more than just a few minutes. The list included the mayor of Greensburg, the City Manager, a young couple with a new baby and numerous other employees.

The CDR men stopped to visit with a few of the many locals coming to the office. The residents were so glad to see that CDR was ready to help. Several names and addresses were gathered together with phone numbers of relatives or friends where the refugees were staying. CDR assured help for the cleanup, but after driving around to check out a few of the new jobs, it was evident that trying to find the address of a house that no longer existed could be a time-consuming process. The job line-ups were mapped out, enabling the big machines to work much more efficiently as they made their way through town. While driving around to inspect the jobs, the workers offered help to homeowners standing around their debris-strewn lots. Almost always, they were very anxious to fill out a work order, once they realized why CDR was there.

By mid-afternoon the group had accomplished what they had set out to do, and headed back to the church in the country to decide how they were going to fulfill the new obligations. The stack of work orders included the addresses of at least thirty-five homes that needed to be demolished.

One contact was a lady whose house had been completely swept away down to the wooden sub-floor. She said that the tornado opened the trunk on her car, rolled the carpet from the house, folding it in half and stuffed it into the trunk. She could not find any of her belongings until she went about a block away and looked on the other side of a partially standing two-story house, where she found a small pile of her things.

CDR arrived in Greensburg Saturday morning with a skid steer, a loader and half a dozen men. They set to work on the house that was the highest priority, and by midday it was pushed to the street. Without too much damage, the foundation was saved.

Next they moved to E. Garfield Street where almost all of the houses were to be removed on both sides of the street for almost a block. A few of the houses were standing, but all needed to be demolished because of severe structural damage. This required some handwork, as there were things in some of the houses that needed to be removed before the equipment took over. During this time, the men kept busy, making contacts around the town and filling out more work orders.

Back in the country at Bethel Church, the phones were ringing constantly and the men were writing up work orders and dispatching crews to the farms and the irrigation, fencing and town crews as fast as they came in.

CDR volunteers came from all over Kansas, Oklahoma, Texas and other parts of US. Some arrived in early the morning after the tornado, and they stuck with us for weeks. Over seven-thousand meals were served at the church that week.

Crews of clean-up workers with their tools just kept walking in. The church doors opened at 7:00 am, and the men were invited to have a drink or snack before they were dispatched to the job sites. Some of them had been on the road all night and some came in the wee hours of the morning and caught a few winks of sleep, rolling out on sleeping bags on the carpet.

There were many faithful behind-the-scenes workers who manned the stations without any fanfare. One of our CDR men in the congregation reported to duty Saturday morning to fill his position, leaving his son's homeless plight to Grandpa. He dispatched crews day after day and was generally depended on for anything that was needed. Even when we ran short of paper towels, he took responsibility. (That was not a minor detail. In one week, we used seven cases of paper towel; a normal year's supply.)

One man took over the generator distribution along with some volunteer electricians; another willing worker oversaw the irrigation repair; and another manned the fencing crews. Many quietly filled in the gaps.

By Saturday night CDR wasn't quite sure where they were headed with everything. A father-and-son team from Montezuma had lined up some maps and went to work organizing jobs. They stuck with the job for weeks. Their list had increased to an astounding sixty-five houses to be removed with potential for much more. It appeared that the only residents who were currently receiving help were those who had friends or relatives living nearby who could assist them with the demolition work. There was a limited amount of volunteers with the equipment to do the job. Together with everyone else, they were quickly finding out that gloves and hand tools weren't going to get the town cleaned up.

On Saturday, CDR also had one excavator, a loader, and a couple dump trucks working in town as a separate crew cleaning up some of the houses of their church members.

Monday morning saw more equipment arriving and unloading at what was once the John Deere dealer. There was soon a loader, a telehandler with grapple, an excavator, a skid steer with grapple and airless tires, two dump trucks, twelve to fifteen men, a John Deer Gator, and a Polaris ranger. Everyone was soon at work on their assigned jobs. By mid-afternoon, they had acquired one or two more skid steers with grapples which were put directly to work. CDR also moved their staging area to a more permanent place, the fenced-in lot to the northeast of the Dillon's grocery store and just off of Hwy 54.

It took two coordinators full time to keep this size of a crew working steadily. CDR quit looking for new work, as enough people had the phone number, and phones were constantly ringing with people wanting help, wondering when work would begin on their property and also calls from volunteers wondering which job to move to next.

The work basically consisted of moving the debris off the foundation and lot into the street where huge piles were gathered for the government to pick up. Many times the foundation was also removed by request of the owner, and CDR's own dump trucks hauled the concrete away when they were available. Many of these foundations are basements. Sometimes the owners also requested that CDR remove the most damaged trees. Very little was salvaged from the houses as almost everything was ruined and the owners had nowhere to go with it if they could save it. If anything of value was found, it was set aside for the owners to sort through, but many times they gave specific instructions to save nothing.

Some of the homeowners told CDR to begin without contacting them, but many times they liked to be there when the demolition began. It was quite emotional, and a few tears would trickle when the equipment began work on their debris.

"It's hard to even imagine what it was like," says Amos Yost, one of the CDR coordinators, "but we did our best to support and encourage them."

The first week, the workers drove out to the church for a lunch of leftovers, but eventually they started eating in town at one of the several locations where groups were providing delicious meals for the volunteers. ATV's drove down the streets to give thirsty volunteers a drink and snack.

KDOT was in charge of all debris removal to one of two dumps. The state had many loaders with grapples loading the piles of debris into waiting trucks.

The army had some equipment on site to do the same thing. As many as 150 trucks or more were hauling debris. All the rubble other than concrete or hazardous material was taken to the north dump where dozers pushed it into the fire. After a few days there was so much debris, that a huge, brand-new D11 Caterpillar dozer was ordered just to keep up. Soon it was as smoky and black as the others.

Chapter 26

Personal Contacts with Victims

One of the most satisfying parts of CDR work was helping people retrieve the belongings they were looking for. The volunteers would lift a wall or a roof or move some debris so that the owners could search for things that were missing. Two pet cats were found two weeks after the tornado in amongst the rubble, much to their owners' delight. It was also enjoyable to visit with the residents. They would tell you exactly where they were hiding during the tornado, and how they survived.

"One elderly man I spoke with had cleaned his entire house, even though it was destroyed," recalls Amos Yost. "When I arrived he was sitting in his arm chair in his living room. The windows were blown out, and the ceiling fan was spinning wildly, due to the wind blowing through the partly missing roof. Those were all the belongings he had left, and he was so appreciative of a visit. He had survived the storm in his neighbor's basement."

The survivors were quick to talk about how very thankful they were to God for protecting them. CDR men enjoyed the time spent with many of the families and friends of the victims of the tornado.

After the first week, the work became more routine. One or two excavators and one or two loaders were kept running every day. Many times the operators teamed up to make it go a little faster. There was so much trouble with rubber tires on the skid steers that they eventually abandoned them. One morning eighteen holes were plugged on a single skid steer's tires! This was not counting all of the other holes that had been plugged during the day. Many brethren brought their equipment, complete with an operator, for a week at a time or longer. CDR eventually rented a Caterpillar excavator to keep on site for the duration of the work.

Volunteers appeared everywhere you turned in Greensburg, and some were contractors. One young man from New York teamed up with CDR for about a week at no charge with a large grapple and truck, made especially for demolition work. The city of Wichita also provided many dump trucks and loaders for a week or two. They had their own contracted tire-repair truck which repaired all CDR's tires for free. There were several other volunteer groups with equipment working in town doing clean up.

CDR concluded the work in town around June 24. Over one hundred houses and foundations had been removed in the one-and-a-half months. Many that were helped had insurance, but some gave a donation in return or gave a donation to another good cause. Those without insurance were not turned away. Sometimes CDR operators took on jobs for pay if they felt like it was out of CDR focus, especially if it was a rental house or business with insurance. CDR figured a cost of $1,000 to remove a house and basement foundation.

By July 1, the city was considered 90% cleaned up. 316,365 yards of debris removed from the town. This is equivalent to 34,095 truck-loads.

There were some extraordinary sights that caused more than one look. The collapsed water tower over the famous, deepest, hand-dug well was one of the destroyed Greensburg landmarks. A hay baler rested on top of the collapsed Fleener's furniture store. A huge oil tank was displaced from near Roger Yost's place, and landed in town, six miles to the north. A pickup was rolled into a ball approximately four feet in diameter, and the banner in front of the auto parts store read, 'Grand Opening.'

The CDR fencing project began May 12, 2007, at Daniel Unruh's place with a few volunteers, mostly youth boys from the area. They worked at the miles of destroyed fence with an admirable persistence. The mangled, twisted wire and broken posts had to be dealt with before the new fence line could be started. Progress seemed slow. Fencing continued almost every day until June 4, completed with the rebuilding of five miles of new fence and the repair of one mile. It was hard but rewarding work, and the men claim to have had some good times!

On June 9, ten Amish men came from Yoder. They brought with them a hydraulic post pounder that drove in not only the fence posts, but also the corner posts!

"In one day they put in over two miles of fence!" exclaimed Craig Yost, who knows just how much work two miles of fencing can be.

CDR irrigation crews worked on the tangle of seven sprinkler systems day after day. There was work to be done everywhere you turned.

Chapter 27

In the Days Following

It would be nice if there were a quick fix when a tornado devastates a community, but unfortunately, there isn't one. In the days immediately following the tornado, the help continued to come. The people of the Greensburg community are deeply indebted to all the many generous organizations and individuals who opened their hearts to them.

The community received $5,300 for CDR in a pile of little checks from a community in Louisiana. So many people care so much! The town of Greensburg really appreciates the help, as it takes $4000 to operate a CDR crew with big equipment for one day. This same Louisiana community had already given CDR $10,000. Perhaps they, too, have suffered trouble at some time and received help.

The ending of the school year had come and gone, but the Valley View Christian School still had not had the school-end play day. A Saturday evening picnic was arranged on Terry and Tamra's yard.

A circle of little girls sat up close to a picnic table deep in serious discussion. "The tornadoes are coming back on Monday and Tuesday!" they said. They clasped their arms around themselves as tight as they could and wiggled with dread.

"Why do you think they're coming back?" they were asked.

"Because the weather monitor says severe weather is coming and conditions will be right for tornadoes again."

Graduation day arrived. Even though the school had suffered damage, it was repaired enough for us to assemble. We looked up at the ceiling and marveled that it had stayed up when the outside wall of the big room gave out. Some of the ladies scooped layers of insulation off the floor, and then ran shop vacuums, but now the stains showed up rather starkly. That sturdy studded wall looked pretty comforting, supporting the structure again. We were glad to have the program in the school so things could be as normal as possible.

The parents of the graduates had their challenges as they prepared the snack with an empty kitchen. Events that would have normally taken detail planning now happened with last-minute preparation. Containers were collected from home and church, and the graduation evening was an enjoyable time.

A neighbor, Ki Gamble, had quite a lot of damage to his house and yard. He backed his stock trailer up to the house to load some furniture, and saw to his dismay that the trailer floor had been sucked out in the storm. He called up David White, another neighbor, to see if he could use his stock trailer. Before he hooked up, he decided to see what the floor looked like in it. No floor there, either; it too, had been sucked out.

The Sewing Center has generously provided towel sets, sheets, and comforters. The congregation is welcome to distribute these items to as many victims in Greensburg as need them. Mennonite Union Aid (MUA) and Brotherhood Auto Aid (BAA) have been generous as well. Christian Public Service (CPS) will set up a unit for young men volunteers to begin helping the community. Recipients of all the services offered have been very grateful.

A month later...

Fear and uncertainty of the weather is yet a common emotion. People not normally fearful are now much more cautious. We ache for the children that feel this uncertainty.

Gradually, they are returning to permanent dwellings. New houses are being built. Some are living in holiday trailers generously donated for such a use. Some have moved into Haviland, and others have made Home Again their permanent residence. Some are still living with others who have generously invited them to temporarily be a part of their family. Some are renting, while others continue to search for permanent housing. A house with boarded-up windows also works to shelter from the elements while the owners wait for new windows. And many have been blessed with a FEMA trailer to live in.

The teacher's house is gaining nicely, with a beautiful job on the cabinetry, built by a volunteer at no labor charge. What a generous labor of love that was! The carpentry crews surely inspired us all when they took hold of our wrecked school and teacher's house. They came, hit it hard and built up our hope as they built up the walls.

Mark Humpage from United Kingdom came back to Greensburg, not as a curious by-passer, but as an active player to the cause of the Greensburg people. His mission over the two days he was here was to capture images of the devastation, talk to the local people, and take the information back home to the UK in order to raise awareness of the event.

Approaching from the south, and a few miles away from Greensburg, evidence of tornado damage was all around. New telegraph poles (117 in a row) replaced damaged, broken trees and isolated property damage both sides of the road. As he entered Greensburg, the same shocking scenes that he witnessed two weeks ago greeted him. For some strange reason he anticipated a whole deal of clean up and a completely different scene. He was wrong. There had been a great deal of clean up, but the shocking scene remained and such was the scale of the disaster.

Continuing around the town he came across every conceivable sight feasible in terms of damage. Some properties flattened to a pile of rubble, others barely standing and some leaving behind just a hole in the ground where the foundations once lay — a truly shocking sight. One such scene he recalls well. All that was left was steps. They were steps that led to nowhere, but a hole in the ground. He couldn't imagine what those residents thought when they returned and this sight greeted them.

Another distressing feature to the array of damage was the countless personal items lying around: shoes, toys and clothes to name a few. These were located in the exact position in which they were left on that May 4 evening after winds had ravaged the town. Quite amazing! One such object was a book. It lay in the dirt next to a concrete foundation where a house once belonged. It was open with the name Karen Smith hand written in the top left corner of the page. Mark's mind went overtime at this point. Was she still alive? Where was she now?

One thing Mark did come across every now and again was a storm shelter. These were effectively steps underground to a basement area, away from the main property. Constructed as a concrete bunker, they were designed to withstand tornadoes and they did save some lives on that night. Most people sought shelter when the warning sirens sounded. However, not everyone can afford such tornado havens and those people who unfortunately lost lives in this disaster either did not have a shelter or chose, for some reason, not to use it.

Another common feature was wrecked cars. The town was littered with cars that looked like they had been sitting on a scrapheap for years. By the looks of them, some cars were obviously picked up and hurled to wherever they landed. Some of them just sat there and looked sad. One of them had a sign wired onto the back: "For Sale. $1.00 or best offer..." This entire event was for sure going to be a gross massive insurance payout.

From a research point of view, Mark was looking for many usual signatures associated with the tornadic damage. These signatures Mark has witnessed before with such damage both in the UK and overseas, albeit in less intense events. Buildings pierced with projectiles, localized rotation damage, bark stripped trees, etc. In fact, so widespread and intense was the destruction that he witnessed very few of these signatures. This shocked him but was also a valuable learning exercise. There comes a point within the rotation destruction of vortexes where damage becomes unrecognizably specific. Maybe this is where and why the EF5 intensity scale was attributed.

Mark Humpage from the UK concludes with, "As they say in the USA, God Bless America."

Over three months later...

Even though there is still much rebuilding in the future, life has taken

146

on more normalcy. Little girls once again sit on front porches playing with their little kitties. Families are catching up the threads of their lives and enjoy happy times again. Fathers pore over new plans for shops, houses, sheds. Of course, an important part of the plans include storm shelters! Money and financial arrangements remain a problem to work out. But they are filled with thankfulness, even though there are unknowns in the future.

Still there are discouraging times. One brother was out walking in a lush, green wheat field one day and saw a piece of paper lying at his feet. He stooped to pick it up. He saw it was a page from someone's Bible. The verses written on the page spoke about Jesus walking on the stormy sea. The message for this man who felt discouraged that day was a message straight from Jesus' own words: Be of good cheer (courage); it is I; be not afraid... It was a very special message sent from God, especially for him.

Over all, there is a caring for each other. This isn't the worst thing that has happened to them, some seniors say. They have experienced other hard times, and know God will carry them through this one, too.

—·—

Over at the school, work is progressing nicely. The starting date has been pushed up a week, and everyone is working hard to make that happen. The teacher's house will be ready for the new teachers.

—·—

Four months later...

It's time to do something that will fill others' needs. The ladies of the sewing circle decide to host the Blood Donor's drive. As they walk in on the appointed day with their pies, one can see the sacrifice they have made. Their own kitchens have been blown away, but their hearts are big and open wide!

Nearly five months later....

Greensburg has a coffee room set up in a storage shed, with tables, chairs, and free coffee five days a week. The community is finding each other, and the tornado aftermath is still the topic of many conversations. Sharing the trauma somehow helps with the acceptance of what has really happened to us, and the healing will be there. Because our public library is still three to five years in the future, a library fund has already put over fifty new books on the shelves in this building. Last week a pot-luck was enjoyed by some of the residents of this town that is slowly coming back to life.

One hundred and sixty building permits have been issued, representing approximately 200-235 people; and there are five hundred people in two hundred mobile homes. These numbers represent almost half the population before the tornado on May 4. Six small businesses are setting up in mobile homes until they can rebuild. There are many new houses going up, and driving across town, you sense a spirit of pioneering as well as survival.

This week we were saddened with the news of the passing of the twelfth Greensburg victim of the tornado, Max McColm.

Norman and Beverly Volz were together the night of the May 4, quietly celebrating the end of Beverly's seven weeks of radiation. At their home that Friday evening, they held hands and smiled. They had been married thirty-three years, and were ready to go ahead with life again.

When they heard the sirens blow, they thought the storm would miss town. Then the power went out, and the wind picked up. Norman tried to open the front door, but couldn't get it open against the wind. "Hallway!" he shouted to Bev, and her father, Max McColm. They scrambled to huddle there.

Suddenly a 15'X 1' piece of metal came hurtling through the house, causing some severe injuries to Bev and her father. Norman suffered a broken kneecap. Norman heard Bev cry out, and they talked back and forth in the rubble. Later he didn't remember what she said, other than that she was in pain. He stumbled out of the house to get help.

Residents got Bev out of the door and into a pickup. She was taken in an ambulance to Dodge City, but her injuries were too severe, and she didn't survive. After the doctors told Norman she was gone, he cried, "What am I going to do without her?"

Sitting in his office at Volz Oil Co., he still looks weary and stunned. Bev's well-fed cats saunter in and out of the office. She loved those cats. Their longtime delivery man, Larry Hoskins (fifty-one), died in the storm that night, too. Larry was single and carefree, loved to hunt and fish and was known to take in stray cats.

Bev's father, Max McColm, was unconscious for a long time, and now, nearly five months later, he has passed away, too.

———◆———

Nurse Patsy Schmidt lives eight miles south of Greensburg. Before the storm, her barn cat, which usually stayed at the barn, clung to the back door. When Patsy heard about the storm coming closer to Greensburg, her heart pounded with anxiousness for her sister and the niece who had just arrived in Greensburg that evening. She headed to town to help victims, and to find her niece, Kim, and her children, Evan (twenty-six months), and Emily (five months.) It took her an hour to reach the edge of town, and walking south on Main, in her uniform, she heard someone calling for help.

A lady, drifting in and out of consciousness, sat in a pickup, quietly suffering. Patsy took off her jacket and placed the clean part around her wound, asking the man with her to apply pressure to the wound. These ladies had known each other for years, but Patsy didn't recognize Beverly. Paramedics soon took over and she continued on her way, looking for her niece and children.

Brenda, Kim's mother, and Kim and the children, had taken shelter in an old cellar. An hour earlier Kim had talked to her husband in Nebraska and told him it was eighty degrees and sunny, but they were in a tornado watch.

"It will be okay," he told her.

The siren wailed on and on, and as they waited by some old fruit shelves, Kim sat crossed legged and nursed her five-month-old baby girl. When the lights went out, and their ears started popping, her mother exclaimed, "That can't be good."

Kim pulled Emily and Evan closer and started praying. They could hear clanging, banging, ripping, and cracking outside. She was afraid that the cracked basement walls would come down on them. Brenda threw a blanket over Evan, and Kim put the baby on a pillow on the floor and then lay on top of her, hoping she wouldn't smother, but wanting to protect her from the fury of the storm.

The house blew away and then debris and rain came down in torrents.

Kim asked her mother, "Are you alive?"

While the children cried, Brenda's response was, "Are you okay?"

As Brenda wriggled free, Kim found out she couldn't move. A slab of a concrete wall lay on top of her. They started to yell for help. Her right shoe was wedged tight, so she pulled her foot out of the shoe, got her right leg up and started moving over onto her right side. Baby Emily was screaming, spattered with mud and debris, but later was found to have only a small cut on her head.

They tried to call 911, but the cell phone wouldn't work. When the wind stopped, they called out for help and soon they saw a flashlight beam. A neighbor stepped down into the rubble and reassured them they would be okay. Kim was in severe pain and rested her head on his knee. She thought her pelvis or legs must be broken from the concrete wall. She couldn't move from the waist down. The rescuer strapped her to a large plank, reassured her that the children seemed to be fine, and then transported her in a pickup to the Dillon triage center. The emergency workers there sent her in an ambulance to Pratt, code red.

———

Later that night, Patsy met her husband, Joel Schmidt, at the Dillon's rescue center. He had been driving in a storm, headed south on HWY 183 when things started to hit the pick-up. Visibility became nil, and his windshield broke. He drove down in a deep ditch on the east side of the highway and parked. He wrapped his coveralls around his head with a prayer, "Lord, if it is my time, here I come."

When things quieted down, he opened the door and glanced back toward Greensburg. He could see the huge tornado moving on its way to Greensburg.

Some storm chasers stopped and checked on him, giving him a ride back into town. He went to his mother's house but there was nothing left of the house except the foundation. Upon finding Patsy at the Dillon's rescue center, Joel asked her, "Have you seen Mother?" No one seemed to know what had happened to their mother, Mabel Schmidt.

———

Mabel, with her brother and sister, had gone to their church basement during the sirens and they were trapped there. Debris filled the stairway. Her brother had lost his one leg years before, but used his strong arms to try to remove the debris. They got to the first landing, and could see light and hear noises outside. They tried to call for help over and over.

In the morning a firefighter with a trained dog heard there might be some missing in that area of town, so he volunteered to help the searchers. This disaster was the first one for the German shepherd dog. He is trained to lead his master to human scent. The dog went to the debris pile and glancing back at the firefighter, began to whine.

Near an opening that turned out to be the blocked stairway, the dog started to descend. As the workers cleared the rubble, they found the three siblings, all unharmed, but glad to be rescued after a twelve-hour wait.

=>·<=

Five months later...

Debby and Farrell Allison sat at a solid wood table in the Haviland library discussing one of the many challenges life has thrown their way lately. They are very much a part of our lives. Farrell walks through our crops, watchful for bugs or moisture, fertilizer and chemical needs, while Debby serves as a very capable librarian.

The Allisons had just completed a barn in their yard and Farrell's parents had not yet seen it. Bob and Dorothy arrived from Texas at 4:30 p.m. on May 4 to pay their children a visit and see the new barn. They hadn't been to Greensburg to see them for two years and enjoyed touring the new barn.

Farrell arrived home from work at 6:00 p.m., telling the last farmer of the day he would be back, south of town, the next morning to help set his planter. That turned out to be a good decision.

The Allison's ate the evening meal together with their parents. Bob Milbern, Farrell's step-father, got up and turned the TV on. They saw the warnings of the tornado. Farrell looked at the radar, and his stomach knotted up. It looked bad to him. He put his boots and hat back on and started to prepare. He got his flashlight and extra batteries. He got some water ready, and while Debby rolled her eyes at his diligence, he even got his Mom's and Debby's medications around. Tornado warnings happen all the time in Kansas, and usually Farrell goes out the door to watch the build-up of clouds.

Now Farrell felt like it was time to proceed to the basement. He didn't have much co-operation from his parents, but he continued to urge them. They don't do steps easily anymore, and were reluctant to go to the basement.

"Maybe if you would carry your mother, Bob would follow you down," Debby suggested to her husband. They finally proceeded downstairs and were down before the siren sounded the warning.

Once they got down the stairs, the ladies wanted to sit on the bed, but Farrell requested the older parents to get under the steps. He pulled a mattress up to cover Debby and himself, drawing as close under the steps as possible.

"Is all this necessary?" Bob questioned Farrell.

"Sit down!" Farrell told him as he put his hands on Bob's chest, pushing him back to safety.

The storm ripped into their house. Huddled down under the stairs, they heard the house creaking and glass shattering as the house yielded to tremendous winds.

That faithful old house had firmly stood for around a hundred years, shaded by old American elm and maple trees. They all gave up together. The elm fell west, across Farrell's mother's car. That house had sheltered the childhood years of their children, and even now it sheltered the four huddled from the storm in the basement. It made a good stand, and though the wind ripped it up to where it was beyond help; it continued to be a shelter for the ones inside.

The fear in Debby's heart wasn't an ordinary fear. She described it as a 'physical fear where the mind blanks out and the body shakes uncontrollably.'

When the storm calmed down a bit, the neighbor lady was at the door. Judy Reed's house and floor had gone, leaving her out in the wind; she was drenched. She had seen her car air-borne and now was very concerned about her son who lived behind Farrell's house. They found a dry shirt for Judy and Farrell made his way up the steps, clearing a path as he went.

"This is bad," Farrell said as he climbed the stairs. One of the first neighbors Farrell found was Judy's son. He had been over to the house, but his mom wasn't there.

Farrell and Debby were so surprised to find all their neighbors alive and uninjured. One of the families was in their basement and a big wooden shelf fell, leaning on the opposite wall. There it sheltered them; the only safe place in their entire house.

Debby marvels at how quickly the neighboring firefighters arrived. Earl Anderson, a former fire chief in Greensburg, drove up from Garden City, and was an excellent help with his experience and knowledge of the town.

A van came from Mullinville to help, offering to help transport Farrell's to Haviland. They arrived at the gym around three o'clock that morning. Denny Ross's, some good friends from rural Haviland, came and picked them up and offered them a home until they found a house in Haviland to buy while they re-build in Greensburg.

Their son, David, and his wife from Tulsa, Oklahoma, were two hours down the road before they knew Farrell and Debby were alive. Having lived in Greensburg for nearly 28 years, it was home to them, too. There is where the children arrived from the hospital, and as their son, David says, "I can come visit you, but I will never again be able to go home." Home: where we cozy into the comforts of life, and the comforts of memories. Home speaks of happy times, and sharing and so many sacrifices to add up to a lifetime of love. The rooms carry the joys for us, even from the past.

———◆◆◆———

Back in Norman Volz's Oil Co. office again, those big cats still ruled the roost, sitting on the laps of the visitors, or keeping toes warm.

Norman was remembering the guard rail that came shooting through the house like a missile. The house had many safe places left, but the missile was uncontrolled and killed his wife and father-in-law. The next evening, he was staying with Scott and Susan Brown in Mullinville and the sirens went off. They decided to drive away in the daylight and found clear skies and sunshine at Bucklin to the west. The clear skies didn't keep the storm at bay for long, so they went on to Ford, and finally holed up in the basement at the Blue Hereford Restaurant.

Norman has found a house in Mullinville for now. A retired couple from CA decided their health doesn't allow them to come back to Kansas anymore, so Norman was fortunate to have a furnished place to move his clothes into and settle in. He said the furniture is there, the bedding was washed up for him, and they even had a jug of iced tea in the fridge and a chocolate cake on the table. He is a thankful person, even though so much in life is sad right now.

———◆◆◆———

Out of life's darkest times, God's love and care shine the brightest. It has been this way for survivors of the Greensburg tornado. However, this experience has left them feeling vulnerable. Most have had to deal with fear following the tornado. Roger Yost was one of them dealing with fear, but he found a victory that he shared with his congregation one Sunday night several months after the tornado.

He said he had read the tract entitled, Free From Fear. This tract had been packed in with the bedding given to the homeless.

"Fear is a tormenting spirit," he said. "It can be a very discouraging factor in our lives if we allow it to take us down that road. The right kind of fear is a healthy fear of God and it brings godly wisdom and humility. This other fear brings about crippling, suffering, and death.

"Satan can trap us in with this fear. It's a part of his scheme. One time the disciples were on the water in a boat and Jesus came walking to them and they began to fear. The waves were boisterous, and they cried out for fear. Jesus reproved them, 'Oh thou of little faith, wherefore didst thou doubt?'

"Fear begins when we doubt. 1 John 4:16-18: *And we have seen and do testify that the Father sent the Son to be the Savior of the world. Whosoever shall confess that Jesus is the Son of God, God dwelleth in him, and he in God. And we have known and believed the love that God hath to us. God is love, and he that dwelleth in love dwelleth in God, and God in him. Herein is our love made perfect, that we may have boldness in the Day of Judgment because as he is, so are we in this world. There is no fear in love but perfect love casteth out fear: because fear hath torment, He that feareth is not made perfect in love.*

"There is no fear in love," Roger continued. "He that fears is not made perfect in love. We that were directly involved that night of the tornado have struggled with this fear to a certain extent. There were ten of us under the steps in our basement. Our son, Terrill and Krista; nephew, Ryan and RaChelle and their two boys; and the four of us were all there. I didn't have any fear at the time. I was in disbelief that it would really happen. When our ears started popping and the house started going, we were audibly praying for God to protect us and keep us. God answered and He was there.

"Many of you had the same experience. It could have been much worse. The battery tank hit the sub floor and put a hole in the floor, but it didn't come through. God's hand was upon us.

"But later on, we became fearful. Storms would come, and to believe that everything would be all right took some faith. We had quite a few sleepless nights.

"When I read this tract, it spoke to me. To me it meant that we would trust and not be faint hearted. We can just have God come to our hearts and put our trust in Him.

"One morning for devotions we read in Isaiah 40:28: Hast thou not known? Hast thou not heard that the everlasting God, the Lord, the Creator of the ends of the earth, fainteth not, neither is weary? There is no searching of his understanding. It was a relief to recognize that God would have a way. At this point we all shed a few tears.

"Life won't be the same anymore. It takes so long to do something now. Work is chaotic. Many friends in town are also experiencing this. But as we think of being free from fear, God wants to take us by the hand. In Deuteronomy 33:27 we read: *The eternal God is thy refuge, and underneath are the everlasting arms: and he shall thrust out the enemy from before thee; and shall say, Destroy them.*

"This is a great comfort. God is there. He cares. He holds us with sustaining arms. Think of the love God has for us, and the undergirding strength. This gives us the ability to trust and look to God in a right way. Fear of the future, fear of failure, wondering how all this will work out troubles us. God showed me the future is there; there can be a reaching out in faith and trust.

"May we look to God. That little world I was holding on to too tightly, too comfortably... it doesn't bring the security we once thought it did. As we look to God, there is hope, there is direction. Fear brings darkness. Satan works in darkness. God is light. There is no darkness with God. There is light at the end of the tunnel.

"That is a beautiful thing God can do for the believer. When a young man thinks of marriage, he reaches forth in faith. It seems light. It seems right. Then looking back, we can see that God was there. He can do the same thing for us in our situation.

"We need to help our children not to fear. They shouldn't be afraid of the dark. If they feel fear in us, they will have it, too. Maybe we can pray with them a simple little prayer asking for Jesus' help. This will give stability. We'll need to be humble enough. The Bible says in the end times men's hearts will be failing them with fear. There is much anxiety. May God lead and guide us is my prayer."

Minister Mark Dirks added: "As little children we learn the verse, I will trust and not be afraid. God wants us to draw closer to Him so we'll be more fit and prepared. It seems like we should be the ones offering Roger our encouragement, but tonight God has had him encourage us. Let's encourage each other. We won't understand everything, but God has a reason and may we trust in Him. If we can't trust God, whom can we trust?

"Let us pray. 'Our Heavenly Father, you have spared our lives, though they are upset and turned around. We know the things of this world are temporal and not lasting. Some day we will stand before you. Help us to cope with fear during these difficult times. We are thankful for the privilege of being together. Go with us in the coming days and be with us wherever we would go. In Jesus' name. Amen.'"

Our Thank You To You

When we realized the immensity of the help and caring shown to us, a thought was born. Some of you have wondered what really happened in our homes the night of May 4. These victims of the tornado have put forth a tremendous emotional effort to write this down as a "Thank-you" for your many kindnesses. May we, in turn, thank God for the great display of strength: strength of nature, strength of prayer, and strength of brotherhood.

How can we adequately thank you for all you've done for us — the material gifts, the tremendous amount of man power (and ladies, too), your equipment used for clean-up, and most of all, your emotional and spiritual support? May God receive all the honor and praise!

We wish each of those involved in the preparation of gifts and services could personally see the homeless receive them. It makes a connection each time we introduce ourselves as from Greensburg, and we hug neighbors we have never hugged before. Hugs to you all!